CONTENTS

Part I
A CHRONICLE OF SPELLS 6

Pyramid Power 10
Magical Controls 13
Circe the Sorceress 14
Seeing is Believing 16
Sacred Spells 18
Hermes Trismegistus, the Thrice-Greatest Wizard 20
Solemn Rites 22
The Cunning Ones 25
Secret Societies 26
Nicolas Flamel and the Philosopher's Stone 28
Modern Wizards 30

★

Part II
PRACTICAL MAGIC 32

The Sorcerer's Apprentice 36
Merlin the Mighty 38
Wicked Words 40
Songs of Enchantment 42
Doctor Dee and Angel Magic 44
A Charmed Life 46
The Wizard's Wand 48
Odin, Master of the Runes 50
Brews and Stews 52
The Magic Mantle 54
Essential Aids 56
Crystal Clear 59
Squaring the Circle 60
Michael Scot and his Magic Travels 62

★

Part III
SPELLS FOR DIFFERENT PURPOSES 64

Sweet Dreams 68
Fata Morgana, Wicked Enchantress 70
Love Charms 72
Fruits of Desire 74
Looks Could Kill 76
George Fitzgerald, the Wizard Earl 78
Healing Charms 80
Crocks of Gold 82
Power and Influence 84
John Dimond and his Granddaughter 86
Dawn Raids 88
Number Magic 90
Days of Reckoning 92
Binding Spells 94

★

PART I

✦

A Chronicle of Spells

*W*izards are as ancient as the human race. As mighty magicians, they possess the power to do what the rest of us can only dream of—to wave a wand and control the path of destiny.

History, myth, and legends are rich in stories of extraordinary individuals, gifted with the awesome ability to shape our world for good or evil. Such god-like beings know no bounds. They can use their magic to travel to other worlds and communicate with spirits there. They can shape-shift into any form they desire, or render themselves invisible. They can read the future.

Wizards are as popular now as they ever were. Our favorite modern spell-casters may be confined to the world of fiction, but the dream lives on. Can you wield the ancient magic?

The WIZARD'S BOOK OF SPELLS

★

THE WIZARD'S
⋆ BOOK OF ⋆
SPELLS

Beatrice Phillpotts
Illustrations by Robert Ingpen

PALAZZO

This edition published in
Great Britain in 2010 by

PALAZZO EDITIONS LTD
2 Wood Street
Bath, BA1 2JQ
United Kingdom

www.palazzoeditions.com

Design and layout copyright © 2010 Palazzo Editions Ltd.
Text copyright © 2010 Palazzo Editions Ltd.

Art Director: Bernard Higton

A CIP catalogue record for this book is available from the
British Library.

ISBN 978-0-95644-484-4

Printed and bound in Singapore by Imago.

ACKNOWLEDGEMENTS

AKG London 10, 11(t), 16, 36(t&b), 41(tl), 50, 60, 82(tl)
AKG London/Erich Lessing 37(t), 77 (centre)
The Art Archive/Eileen Tweedy 88
The Art Archive/Victoria & Albert Museum London/Sally Chappell 85
reproduced by the permission of Hodder & Stoughton Publishers
Bridgeman Art Library 1(t) Natural History Museum; 4(t) British
Library, London; 4(br) Rafael Valls Gallery; 5(br) San Diego Museum
of Art; 11 The Fine Art Society, London; 12 Yale Center for British Art;
14 Oldham Art Gallery; 17(tl) Private Collection; 18(tl) National Gallery
of Scotland, Edinburgh; 18(br) Private Collection; 19(br) Private
Collection; 19(tr) Private Collection; 23(br) Duomo, Umbria/Giraudon;
25 Musee des Beaux-Arts, Lille/Lauros-Giraudon; 30 Delaware Art
Museum, Wilmington, USA; 38 Bibliotheque des Arts Decoratifs,
Paris/Archives Charmet; 40/41(b) British Library, London; 42(r)
Christie's Images, London; 43 Private Collection © The Arthur Rackham
Pictures are reproduced with the kind permission of his family; 44
Private Collection; 46 Ashmolean Museum, Oxford; 47 Museo Lazaro
Galdiano, Madrid; 48/49 National Gallery of Scotland, Edinburgh; 52(tl)
Christie's Images, London; 53(br) National History Museum, London; 55
Private Collection; 57(l) Galleria dell'Accademia Carrera, Bergamo;
57(r)Alan Jacobs Gallery; 58 Manchester Art Gallery; 61(b) Private
Collection; 62 Johnny van Haeften Gallery; 68(t) National Gallery of
Scotland, Edinburgh; 68(b) Warrington Museum and Art Gallery; 69
The Maas Gallery; 70 Birmingham Museums and Art Gallery; 72
Kunsthaus, Zurich; 72(bl) Royal Botanical Gardens, Kew; 72(br)
Fitzwilliam Museum, Cambridge; 73 The De Morgan Centre, London;
74(l) The Fine Art Society, London; 74(b) Victoria & Albert Museum,
London; 75 Bibliotheque Nationale, Paris; 76(l) British Museum,
London; 77 Victoria Art Gallery, Bath; 78 State Library of New South
Wales; 80(b) O'Shea Gallery, London; British Library, London; 82(bl)
British Library, London; 83(tl) Musee des Beaux-Arts,
Valenciennes/Lauros-Giraudon; 83(br) Roy Miles Fine Paintings; 84(l)
Birmingham Museums and Art Gallery; 86 Ashmolean Museum, Oxford;
92(l) Private Collection; 94(tr) York Museums Trust (York Art Gallery)
Fortean Picture Library 17(br), 20, 27(l), 41, 44(bl), 61(t)
Mary Evans Picture Library 5, 12, 23, 24, 26, 31, 40, 52(br), 53(bl),
80(tl), 84(r), 90
Robert Ingpen 2, 7, 8, 15, 21, 29, 33, 34, 39, 45, 51, 54, 59, 63, 65, 66, 71,
79, 87, 89, 94, 96

p. 30 and 48 Excerpts from *A Wizard of Earthsea* by Ursula K. Le Guin.
Copyright © 1968, 1996 by The Inter-Vivos Trust for the Le Guin
Children. Reprinted by permission of Houghton Mifflin Company.
All rights reserved.
p. 31 *The Subtle Knife* by Philip Pullman copyright © Philip Pullman 1997,
the second book in his *The Dark Materials* trilogy, published by Scholastic
Children's Books and reproduced by permission of Scholastic Ltd.

Every effort has been made to contact
copyright holders. If any omissions do
occur, the publisher would be pleased
to give full credit in subsequent
reprints and editions.

PYRAMID POWER

In the world of the ancient Egyptians, magic was all-important and permeated every aspect of their civilization: it was believed to be essential energy created before life began and to possess power over death itself.

The great magic of ancient Egypt was a sacred science and its workings were revealed only to an elite of scribes. These all-powerful magicians were the wizards of their day. Their books of magic, many of which have been preserved to this day, enjoyed a life of their own because they were written in hieroglyphs—signs that were believed to possess a living force.

The magic spells written in hieroglyphs on the inner walls of the pyramids of the Old Kingdom, dating from between c. 2650 and c. 2190 BC, were regarded as living entities. They reinforced the powers of the pharaohs buried within, themselves worshipped as "magician kings." Death was no obstacle to a pharaoh: filled with magic and armored with spells, he conquered death and lived on forever in the Egyptian afterlife.

While pharaohs were born as magical beings, lesser mortals had to be initiated in the art of magic. A would-be wizard could not simply read magical texts in order to learn his art, he must literally swallow the words. The pieces of papyrus bearing the spell or incantation were put in a bowl of water to soften, and then the words were actually drunk.

Once filled with magic in this way, a wizard became a god-like being, able to exercise power over evil that threatened the natural order of life. The magic within a wizard was like a living force and was a sensory experience. It was as visible as rays of light shining from him and could even be smelled.

"Behold, I am one with that magic power, wheresoever it may be, in the house of any man where it is," pronounced the wizard in Spell 24 of the ancient Egyptian "Book of the Dead." "It is faster than the hare, swifter than light."

The most famous wizard of the Old Kingdom was Imhotep, a wise man and scholar who lived around 2600 BC and who held the position of first minister to the mighty pharaoh Djoser. Imhotep was powerful enough to invoke a god, if he so desired, using the following magical procedure that has been passed down to us:

"Take an olive wood table with four feet. Place it in the center of a pure place: cover it completely with a cloth. Place four bricks beneath the table, one on top of the other, and in front of the table, a silver censer. Put charcoal made from olive wood in the censer and goose fat minced with myrrh and shaped into small dumplings, and recite a spell. Speak to no one throughout the night. You will see the god in the form of a priest dressed in a linen robe."

MAGICAL CONTROLS

The god-like wizards of ancient Egypt were believed to be made of earth, air, fire, and water, and they wielded power over these four elements. When fire or flood threatened to destroy the natural order of their world, for example, they could use their powerful magic to restore the equilibrium.

The lords of all they surveyed, these wise men could cast spells to disperse the shadows and allow the life-giving rays of the Sun to shine down. This kind of magic had to be renewed each day; to do this, the papyrus leaf bearing the appropriate spell had to be shut inside a box and thrown daily into a fire prepared for this purpose.

Protected by strong magic, the wizards of ancient Egypt could travel into the kingdom of the dead and drink the miraculous water found therein. This precious liquid bestowed upon the wizard even greater powers. This is the spell from the ancient Egyptian "Book of the Dead," to be uttered just before drinking. It is an appeal to Nun, goddess of the primeval ocean, who has the power to make the gift:

"Come to me each day, you who are the waters of rejuvenation! Refresh my heart with the fresh water of your stream! Grant that I may have power over water like She who is Powerful!"

Apocalyptic visions of a great flood of water, visited upon the Earth as a punishment for the sins of mankind, feature in myths and legends all over the world. A common theme in these tales is the intervention of a divine or magical being to ensure that the destruction is not total and that from the disaster seeds of a better life will grow.

In a Native American version of the flood myth, a chance meeting with a sorceress saves one lucky man from drowning and enables him to become the patriarch of the new human race.

One day this man—a farmer by trade—wakes to discover that every tree he felled the day before has magically grown again. This happens on subsequent days, until one night the farmer decides to stay up and watch how this miracle occurs. He sees an old woman rise up from the ground; she makes certain movements with her wand and the felled trees spring up again. When he confronts her, the sorceress warns him that the world is about to be destroyed by a great flood, but that she can protect him with her magic.

Following her instructions, the farmer makes a coffin out of a fig tree. He collects five grains of each color of corn, some fire, five squash stems to burn, and a black bitch and shuts himself inside the coffin with these items. The old woman sits on top with a parrot on one shoulder and a macaw on the other and they ride the great flood for five years. When the flood subsides, the sorceress releases the two birds, who excavate vast river valleys with their beaks to drain the remaining water, and the farmer's canine companion is magically revealed to be a young woman. The fortunate couple produce a large family, plant corn, and live happily ever after.

CIRCE THE SORCERESS

"Who knows not Circe,
The daughter of the Sun, whose charmed cup
Whoever tasted, lost his upright shape,
And downward fell into a grovelling swine?"

*T*he beautiful magician Circe is best known for transforming the legendary Odysseus's men into pigs during their fateful visit to her enchanted island, an episode recorded by the seventeenth-century English poet John Milton in "The Masque of Comus."

Fortunately for the twenty-two men who fell under her evil spell on that occasion, Circe's magic was successfully resisted by Odysseus with the help of a flowering onion, allium moly, which had been given to him especially for that purpose by the Greek god Hermes. Defeated, the enchantress agreed to restore Odysseus's men to him. "Circe went to the swine pen and anointed each of the swine that was there with a charm. As she did, the bristles dropped away and the limbs of the men were even taller and handsomer than they had been before," recounted the ancient Greek poet Homer in his epic tale "The Odyssey."

Others were not so lucky; most people who visited Circe's island were bewitched after they had feasted at her magic banquet and the sorceress had struck them with her wand. Men changed into beasts—mainly swine—and women were transformed into monsters, particularly snakes. It was said, however, that even in their enchanted states, these people retained the ability to reason. They were fed on the fruit of the cornel tree, red berries that were thought to be the food of the dead.

The daughter of the Sun god Helios, Circe had hair so red it resembled flames. Her mother was rumored to be Hecate, the patron goddess of magic. According to Homer, Circe controlled fate and the forces of creation

and destruction by knotting her hair into braids. The tying and untying of knots is used to bind and release energy in many spells.

According to legend, at night Circe's chamber was filled with spirits and her magic was so powerful that she could make trees move and turn white. The enchantress could also cause the ground to quake beneath her as she walked.

Those who crossed the evil Circe lived to regret it, even if they were deities themselves. When the demi-god Picus spurned Circe, she changed him into a woodpecker and when the sea god Glaucus fell in love with the sea nymph Scylla rather than herself, Circe retaliated by changing Scylla into a monstrous serpent.

CIRCE

SEEING IS BELIEVING

*S*hape-shifting is the ultimate magical weapon and wizards are some of the best practitioners of this art. They are not only able to change their own appearance, they can also change another person's form through magical means.

God-like wizards automatically possess miraculous powers of transformation. The great magicians of myth and legend often defeated their foes by transforming themselves into demonic monsters, fearsome birds, or giant fish; sometimes they even made themselves invisible.

Odin, the Norse god of war, was a mighty magician. Worshipped as a creator god by the Vikings, his cult reached its zenith in the eighth and ninth centuries AD. Like Varuna, the Hindu sky god, Odin ruled by means of magic.

Famed as a shape-shifter, Odin's powers apparently knew no bounds. One of his most chilling legendary exploits was transforming himself into a corpse in order to learn the secrets of the world. He hung, as if dead, from the World Tree for nine days and nine nights to discover knowledge that was kept secret from the living. He succeeded and, finding himself imbued with even greater wisdom than he had previously known, Odin cast off death and resumed his normal form.

The most fearsome weapon in the shape-shifter's arsenal is the power he or she has to become invisible. Traditionally, this gift was bestowed in the form of magical clothing. The gift of invisibility was granted to the ancient Greek hero Perseus in the form of a magic cap. Wearing it enabled him to escape from his murderous pursuers, the two Gorgons, after he had killed their sister, the monster Medusa. In J. K. Rowling's "Harry Potter and the Philosopher's Stone," modern wizard Harry Potter receives the ultimate Christmas present—an invisibility cloak. The cloak comes with the warning that he must use it as a force for good. He is overwhelmed by this mysterious gift.

When Harry unwraps his exciting parcel, he discovers a shining, silvery cloth that is light and almost fluid to the touch. Once on, the cloak seems to flow over him. Hidden within its magical folds, he and his friends are able to pass through the many passageways in Hogwarts School unseen. Rendered invisible, they reach the secret trapdoor that hides the all-powerful Philosopher's Stone unchallenged.

Wizards frequently assume the form of an animal. Experts believe they have found evidence of the activities of the earliest-known wizards in Britain, based on a deer-skull mask excavated in Yorkshire in England and dating from around 700 BC.

Shape-shifting could also be used to change beasts into beauties to dupe unsuspecting humans. Mortals could sometimes reverse the powerful magic; this occurs in the famous fairy tale "Beauty and the Beast," in which a beautiful young woman manages to break the spell that has transformed a handsome prince into a monster.

The power of love triumphs, too, in the ancient Scottish ballad "Young Tam Lin." The hero Tam Lin has had a shape-shifting spell cast on him causing him to assume many fearsome guises, but asks his sweetheart to hold him tight despite his frightening appearance. She does so, and the spell is broken:

"They'll turn me in your arms, lady,
Into esk and adder;
But hold me fast, and fear me not
I am your bairn's father.

They'll turn me to a bear sae grim,
And then a lion bold;
But hold me fast, and fear me not,
As ye shall love your child."

The mask is thought to have been worn by a wizard to enable him to change into a deer. It was believed that the wizard would then be able to enter the animal's psyche, gaining information that would guarantee success in the next deer hunt.

believed to act as bridges between the two realms of land and sky, transmitting water between them. Nature, and trees in particular, played a central role in Druid wizardry.

Druids believed that mistletoe contained the power to heal any ailment, but in order to do so it had to be harvested from a sacred oak on the sixth day of the Moon by a Druid with a golden sickle and caught by virgins garbed in pure-white cloth. Clad in flowing white robes, the Druids used wooden staffs made from yew and engraved with magical Ogham characters to help conduct their magic; yew symbolized death and rebirth in the cycle of life.

A Druid had the power to cast a spell that would incapacitate not just an individual, but

*M*embers of the priestly class of the ancient Celts were known as Druids and they were revered as mighty sorcerers. Being a Druid involved a lifelong training. A child was selected for initiation because he or she was believed to possess spiritual powers, and the training continued for more than thirty years. A fully fledged Druid was both a high priest and an important advisor to the leader. The cult died out in Britain in the first century AD but was revived in the eighteenth century. There are now nearly twenty orders practicing pantheistic nature worship, notably at the annual celebration of the summer solstice at Stonehenge in England. The most powerful wizards of their day, Druids were known as "the very wise ones." They possessed extraordinary powers and could employ them to protect lesser mortals from evil spirits and to forecast future events. They devised a secret language that included a tree alphabet—or Ogham—which could be used to cast spells. Trees were sacred to the Druids because they were

an entire army. According to legend, in one Irish battle fought in AD 561, the king called upon the Druid Fraechan to create a magic fence to protect his southern army, which then successfully defeated 3,000 enemy soldiers.

Mistletoe Spell for Luck

"With a consecrated ritual dagger, ceremonially cut a piece of mistletoe on winter solstice. As you do this, recite thrice: 'Golden bough and Witch's broom, thy sacred names are spoken. By dagger's blade I conjure thee to see all bad luck broken. harming none, this spell is done. By law of three, so mote it be!' hang the mistletoe over your front door. It will bring good luck to all who dwell within."

Irish legend is full of vivid descriptions of Druids wielding their magic powers to change the course of events. Occasionally they found themselves on opposing sides, if they were working to help rival rulers. The consequences of these wizards working against each other could be earth-shattering: a pitched battle between a mighty Druid working for the north and an equally mighty Druid working for the south is described in the ancient Irish "Book of Leinster."

In a fit of anger, the northern wizard Ciothrue dried up all the wells in the southern province, but the wizard Mog Ruth drove a silver tube into the ground and a spring burst forth to replenish them. Ciothrue then made a fire and cast a spell with his magic rod that summoned a black cloud and a shower of blood rained down on the south. Mog Ruth retaliated by transforming three of Ciothrue's fellow northern Druids into stones.

Dark clouds, or magic mists, were an important part of the Druid's arsenal. It is said that the Irish wizard Mananan summoned a magical mist to lead King Cormac to his hut, where he apparently treated the ruler to a pork supper in the assumed form of a young man, as a gesture of good will.

HERMES TRISMEGISTUS, THE THRICE-GREATEST WIZARD

*A*ll-powerful Hermes Trismegistus was actually a mythological being born of two gods of magic; he is also the historical founder of alchemy, the ultimate wizard's art.

Fruit of the mystical union of the Greek god Hermes and the Egyptian god Thoth, the mighty mythic wizard Hermes Trismegistus is believed to have composed a vast volume of writings in the time of Moses. Known as the "Hermetic Texts," this is said to have consisted of forty-two books. These books have profoundly influenced the development of western magic.

The greatest of these books, "The Emerald Tablet," imparts the magical secrets of the Universe, and the text is believed originally to have been inscribed on an emerald belonging to the wizard. Legend tells how Sarah, wife of the patriarch Abraham, discovered this volume in Hermes Trismegistus's cave tomb. Most of the other volumes of the "Hermetic Texts" were believed to have been housed in the famous royal library at Alexandria and destroyed in the great fire of 97 BC. Mystery shrouds the whereabouts of any surviving volumes. Some say that they have been buried in a secret location in the desert and that they will be discovered when the time is right.

The wizard's surviving wisdom has been passed down through the centuries and many subsequent spells and rituals have been based upon his works. The riddle-like opening sentence of "The Emerald Tablet" sets out his belief that man possesses the power to be godlike:

"*T*hat which is above is like that which is below and that which is below is like that which is above, to achieve the wonders of the one thing."

His parents, Thoth and Hermes, were also associated with magical writings. Indeed, their prodigious output makes the creative outpouring of their wizard offspring seem quite scanty. Incredibly, Hermes is believed to have dictated 20,000 books to the Syrian philosopher Iamblichus, who lived around 300 BC, and a further 36,000 books to the philosopher's contemporary, the Egyptian priest Manetho.

As scribe to the gods, however, Thoth must be pre-eminent. He was, quite simply, credited with the authorship of all sacred books: "I am Thoth, master of divine words, he who acts as interpreter to all the gods," he proudly declared.

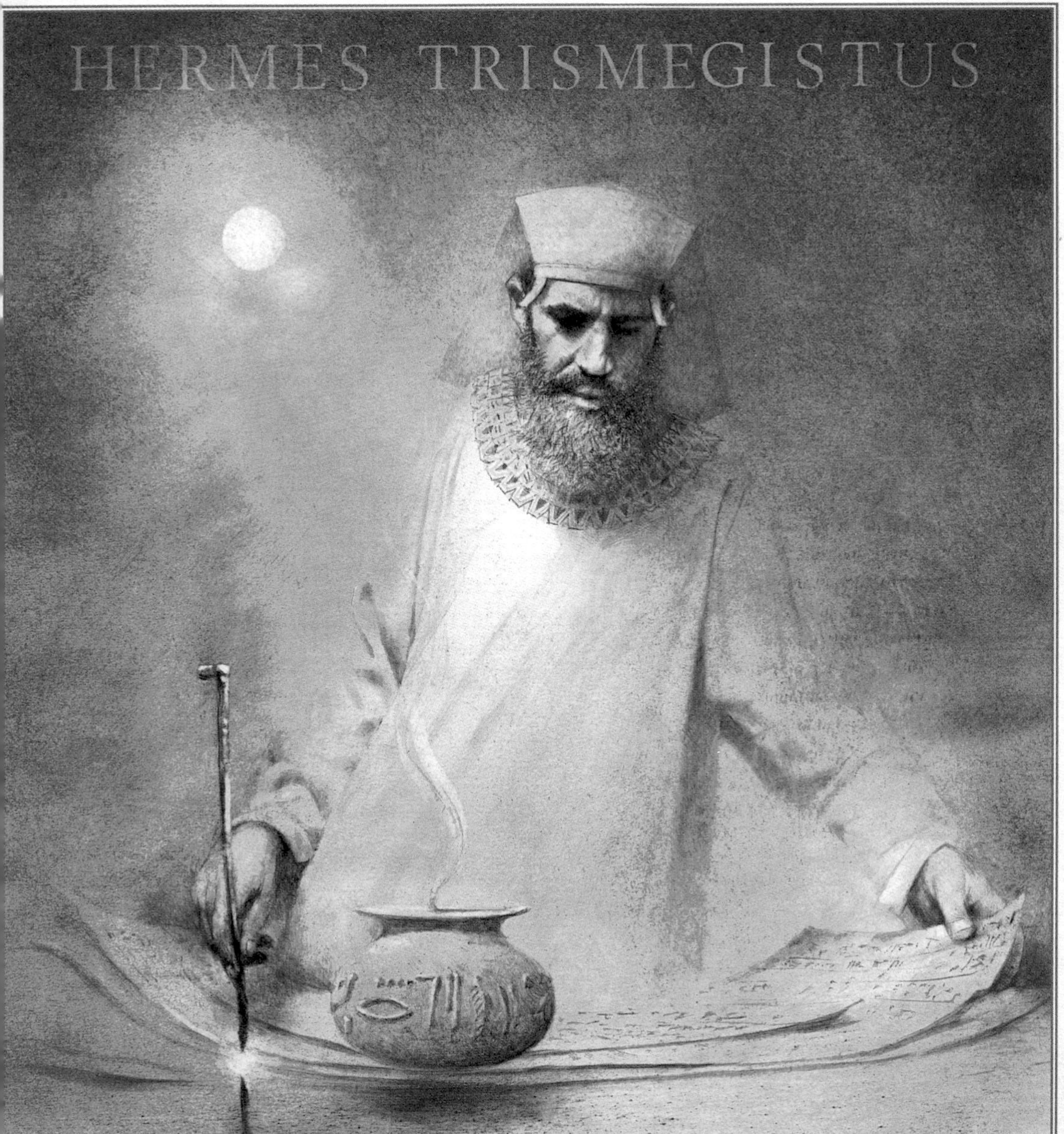
HERMES TRISMEGISTUS

SOLEMN RITES

*I*nterest in magic scaled new heights during
the Renaissance. Distinguished scholars insisted
that the study of "natural magic" was vital for
a true understanding of Christianity, and
they devised a complex system of natural
magic based on the Cabala.

Magical applications of the Cabala, a
mystical interpretation derived from the very first sacred
writings of the Jews, were recognized as early as the
thirteenth century. During the Renaissance, alchemists and
magicians used combinations of Cabalistic numbers and
divine names in complex rituals and incantations.

Cornelius Agrippa, a sixteenth-century German wizard,
studied the Cabala and incorporated it into his important
three-volume work on magic, "On Occult Philosophy." He
maintained that magic had nothing to do with the Devil,
but rather depended upon natural psychic gifts. It was
popularly believed, however, that he practiced necromancy.

Agrippa's awesome magical powers were celebrated in a
legend concerning the death in mysterious circumstances of
his lodger. The young man borrowed the key to Agrippa's
study from his wife in the magician's absence—with
terrifying consequences. In the study the lodger found a
book of magic spells and made the mistake of reading one
aloud. There was instantly a knock on the door and a
demon appeared, demanding to know why he had been
summoned. The lodger was too frightened to reply,
whereupon the demon strangled him. Agrippa was horrified
to discover the corpse in his house and summoned the
demon to restore his lodger to life. The young man was
successfully reanimated, but on leaving the house he
collapsed and died. The marks of strangulation were found
on his body and Agrippa was accused of murder. The
wizard fled town and successfully avoided prosecution.

The complex studies of esoteric branches of science,
astrology, mathematics, and medicine to enable Renaissance
wizards to practice their craft gave rise to equally intricate
magical procedures. Successful spell-casting could only be
accomplished by observing special ceremonial rites. The
correct robes had to be worn, their tools had to be
consecrated, and particular magic symbols
employed and sacred names of power invoked.
The solemn rites were conducted within a
protective magic circle.

The elaborate rites involved in ceremonial magic,
however, empowered wizards to enter a transcendental
realm in which they could summon spirits to do their
bidding. These were usually demons, as they were believed
to be easier to control than angels.

Demon-summoning was accomplished most famously by
the legendary Doctor Faustus, who used his magic arts to
make a pact with the Devil. The Devil taught Faustus the
secrets of the Universe and all the magic he cared to know.
He even allowed the doctor to ride him on revelatory
journeys around the world. In return for these favors,
however, he required Faustus's soul. When the agreed time
had passed, the Devil descended in a terrible wind at
midnight to collect his dues and the mangled remains of
Faustus, scattered around his home, were discovered by
shocked neighbors the following morning.

Others were less concerned with the darkness of personal
gain, however. The scholarly Elizabethan magician Doctor
John Dee devoted most of his life to trying to communicate
with angels. He commissioned the help of fellow alchemist
and medium Edward Kelley and used a secret language he
had invented, Enochian. Dee claimed to have successfully
summoned Uriel, the angel of light written of in the
Cabala, and the archangel Michael.

THE CUNNING ONES

Scholar wizards were also known as "cunning men" and "cunning women." They, too, employed elaborate rituals in order to cast their spells. However, they were also born with psychic powers and they channeled their own energies to miraculous effect.

Traditionally, the cunning ones were the resident magicians of small towns and villages and they were paid by members of the community to practice magic on their behalf. Such country wizards were much in demand: "A Cunning-Man, or a Cunning-Woman, as they are termed, is to be found near every town," noted the British poet Robert Southey in 1807.

The famous British cunning man James Murrell was born in 1780. He was the seventh son of a seventh son, and was thus a wizard by birth. He used manuals of magic to supplement his own psychic powers and his skills were sought not only by locals but also by wealthy and aristocratic clients. Murrell charged a shilling for low magic pertaining to the material world and up to half a crown for high magic, which involved summoning spirits.

Murrell was gifted with second sight and divined with the aid of a magic mirror. He was an expert at casting witch-bottle spells to protect against evil spirits. His witch bottles were fashioned from iron by the local blacksmith and then enchanted by the wizard to produce the required results.

One of Murrell's best-known spells was cast to counteract a witch's curse. He was commissioned to cure a young woman who suffered fits, during which she acted alternately as a cat or a dog; these fits were the result of a curse placed upon her by a drunken old woman who she had evicted from the family barn. Murrell filled a witch bottle with a magical concoction composed of the girl's urine and blood, herbs, and pins. To effect the magic he then heated the bottle on a fire, in a darkened room, behind locked doors, and in absolute silence.

As he was heating the mixture there came a furious knocking at the door and a woman's voice shouted "For God's sake, stop! You're killing me." The bottle exploded and the voice faded away. The girl was cured and the badly burnt body of the old woman who had cursed her was discovered lying in the road three miles away.

The cunning ones were credited with powerful healing abilities. The nineteenth-century Irish healer Biddy Early was widely believed to be "of the fairies" and also used a magic bottle to cure her clients. Early's mysterious dark bottle had apparently been presented to her by the fairies. By looking into it with one eye while keeping the other eye open, she was able to see what ailed her client and was also able to look into the future. Occasionally she used her magic bottle to help clients who were being persecuted by the fairies, usually because they had inadvertently disturbed them. This did not go down well with the fairies, though. Early admitted that they gave her a terrible "grueling" for working against them.

SECRET SOCIETIES

The complicated rituals favored by scholarly Renaissance wizards reinforced the ancient belief that magic was a high art, veiled in mysteries that could only be penetrated by a secret elite of adepts.

Members of secret magical orders, such as the Rosicrucians, conducted increasingly elaborate ceremonies in the seventeenth and eighteenth centuries and consulted esoteric handbooks of magic for guidance on how to summon the most appropriate demons and spirits. The most popular handbook of the day was "The Key of Solomon." Attributed to the legendary King Solomon—who was believed to have commanded an army of demons—it was full of summoning spells.

Ceremonial magic flourished in the nineteenth century and led to the formation of an influential new wizarding movement, the Hermetic Order of the Golden Dawn. Founded by three Rosicrucians in England in 1888, it was based on an old German occult order and had an elaborate hierarchy. This consisted of ten grades, each divided into three orders, with an eleventh grade for novices. Initiates advanced through the Outer Order by examination, but the Second Order had only three members, who were the movement's founders. These three claimed to work under the direction of the Secret Chiefs of the Third Order, who were spirits of the astral plane.

Aleister Crowley, the most notorious British wizard of the early twentieth century, became a member of this movement but was expelled by one of its chief magicians, who was so annoyed by Crowley that he apparently dispatched an army of spirits to attack the wizard. Undeterred, Crowley founded his own movement, The Abbey of Thelema. It was based on "The Book of the Law," which he claimed had been dictated to him by Aiwass, the magical energy force worshiped by the ancient Egyptians as Seth.

Crowley called himself The Great Beast 666, and believed he was the reincarnation of several powerful wizards, including the Elizabethan occultist John Dee. Like Dee, Crowley used Enochian magic to explore the astral plane and he wrote many descriptions of his magical visions.

In one, experienced as his alter ego The Master Therion, Crowley met an "infinitely wise" wizard, who showed him a magical egg set within the four elements and informed him that it contained the secrets of life itself. In his autobiography, Crowley claimed to have seen as many as 316 demons in one evening.

Crowley's beliefs paved the way for the new-age movement Wicca, which is one of the fastest-growing religions in the United States today. Wiccans, like Crowley, practice magick rather than magic. The "k" is added to differentiate their practices from the "magic" of stage entertainment.

Wiccans are guided by the central principle "an it harm none, do what ye will." Most Wiccans worship some form of the Earth goddess and try to live in harmony with Nature. They celebrate the passing of the seasons and hold special ceremonies to mark key transitions in the cycle of life. The spells they cast include this procedure to help anyone in need of protection:

First, a magickal protection oil is made by mixing 1/8 cup of jojoba or almond oil, four drops of pettigrain oil and one drop of clove oil. The spell is cast by charging the oil, by means of visualizing the energy leaving one's own body, and infusing the oil, while chanting:

"I stand here in your guardian light,
Empower this oil with your might.
Protection from harm is what I ask,
Please accept this as your task."

NICOLAS FLAMEL AND THE PHILOSOPHER'S STONE

For hundreds of years, alchemists have pored over magical texts and studied medicine, science, and astrology in order to create the Philosopher's Stone. The ultimate magical elixir, the Philosopher's Stone was reputed not only to possess the power to transform base metals into gold, but also to bestow everlasting life.

Medieval scholars believed that the secret of the Philosopher's Stone had originally been unlocked and set down by the wizards of ancient Egypt. Legend has it that the fourteenth-century French alchemist Nicolas Flamel obtained the magical text and with its help, achieved the seemingly impossible: he transformed mercury into gold and in doing so achieved immortality.

Flamel lives on, as readers of "Harry Potter and the Philosopher's Stone" by J. K. Rowling, well know and due to this the medieval French alchemist has achieved fresh notoriety. It was Flamel's Philosopher's Stone that the evil wizard Voldemort tried but failed to steal, thanks to Harry Potter's heroic intervention. Harry is also delighted to learn that Flamel is still alive, living in Devon with his wife Perenelle, and has just celebrated his six hundred and sixty-fifth birthday.

The real Nicolas Flamel was born in 1330. He lived and worked in Paris as a bookseller and a copier of documents. His unremarkable life changed dramatically one night when an angel visited him in a dream and told him that he would receive a miraculous book that he must strive to understand in order to gain extraordinary powers.

The dream came true, as Flamel recorded in his manuscript "Livres des figures hyeroglyphiques":

"There fell into my hands for the sum of two florins, a guilded Book, very old and large. It was not Paper, nor of Parchment, as other Books be, but was only made of delicate rinds of tender young trees. The cover of it was of brass, well bound, all engraven with letters, or strange figures.... It contained thrice—seven leaves, for so were they counted in the top of the leaves, and always every seventh leaf was without any writing; but, instead thereof, upon the first seventh leaf, there was painted a Rod and Serpents swallowing it up."

The mysterious document was entitled "Book of Abraham the Jew" and it took Flamel twenty-one years of traveling and research before he could decipher it. Eventually with the help of a Hebrew scholar, Flamel was able to create his own Philosopher's Stone. The magical moment occurred on April 25 in 1382, as he recorded:

"Following always my Book, from word to word, I made projection of the Red Stone upon the like quantity of Mercury ... which I transmuted truly into almost as much pure Gold, better assuredly than common Gold, more soft and more plyable."

Anxious not to abuse his miraculous gift, Flamel claimed he had only created gold three times and used his new-found wealth to help found hospitals, chapels, and churches. Empowered by the Philosopher's Stone, he and his wife live on. Prior to the sighting in Harry Potter, they were apparently spotted in India in the seventeenth century, according to the contemporary French archaeologist Paul Lucas.

NICOLAS FLAMEL

MODERN WIZARDS

Today's best-known wizards are the heroes and heroines of fantasy fiction, but even these are firmly based on the exploits of a long line of both real and legendary spell-mongers. These modern wizards have kindled a new enthusiasm for the world of magic.

The archetypal twentieth-century fictional wizard is Gandalf, the guiding spirit in the heroic quest that unfolds in the three companion volumes that created the entire fantasy genre—*The Lord of the Rings*" by the British author J. R. R. Tolkien. Now commanding an even larger following due to the immense popularity of the recent films of the book, the character of Gandalf was inspired by Tolkien's detailed knowledge and love of early myth and legend. A professor of Anglo-Saxon and English language and literature, Tolkien used his expert skills and powerful imagination to create a whole new magical world, Middle Earth, in which Gandalf is a driving force for good against evil.

An old man with a white beard and a tall hat, Gandalf carries a magic staff and wears the Red Ring of Fire. He is a wizard who has shaped many later magical heroes, notably Ursula Le Guin's wizard Ged, who similarly battles great evil in *"The Earthsea Quartet"*:

> "Be thou made whole!' Ged said in a clear voice and with his staff he drew in lines of fire across the gate of rocks a figure: the rune Agnen, the rune of Ending."

A very different wizard—but an equally powerful force for good—is featured in the enormously popular "Star Wars" movies, conceived by American director George Lucas. While Tolkien's battle against evil is fought on Earth, Lucas transports us into deep space for his clash of good against evil, characterized by the Force. His wizard guide is an ancient sprite-like creature called Yoda. Harking back to the ancient Egyptian belief in magic as a supreme creative energy, Yoda is a master of an elite group, the Jedi, who have learned to control the Force and thus possess superhuman powers which are used against the Dark Side.

Prize-winning contemporary British author Philip Pullman creates a shaman as a central character in his magical trilogy *"The Dark Materials."* Pullman's shaman, Doctor Grumman, guides the American astronaut Lee Scoresby's hot-air balloon through a secret opening into a parallel world. He then empowers Scoresby to fly like a bird alongside his own eagle spirit Sayan Kotor in order to defeat the forces of evil:

to vanquish evil before he has even completed his formal magical education. Harry Potter, the wizard hero of British author J. K. Rowling's series of books, has captured the public imagination to such an extent that the stories have become a publishing phenomenon.

In Rowling's unfolding drama, Harry is pitted against the mighty Dark wizard Lord Voldemort in each new adventure. Voldemort's evil magic had killed both his parents but it had failed to destroy Harry, even though he was just a baby in his mother's arms at the time. Indeed, so strong was Harry's magical aura that it almost destroyed his fearsome opponent.

Harry represents a new style of wizard, but he is guided by an archetypal older and wiser wizard, Professor Dumbledore, similar to Merlyn in T. H. White's "The Sword in the Stone":

"Lee felt whatever bird—nature he was sharing respond with joy to the command of the eagle queen, and whatever human—ness he had left felt the strangest of pleasures: that of offering eager obedience to a stronger power that was wholly right."

The world's best-known modern wizard, however, is not an adult but an extraordinary boy, who is powerful enough

"Merlyn had a long white beard and long white moustache which hung down on either side of it, and close inspection shewed that he was far from clean ... some large bird seemed to have been nesting in his hair.... his mild blue eyes very big and round under the tarantula spectacles, gradually filmed and clouded over as he gazed at the boy."

PART II

★

PRACTICAL MAGIC

*W*hat are the essential aids of the successful wizard? Magic is a complicated business. A spell can be cast in many different ways but it will fail if the time-honored rules are not obeyed.

The greatest wizards may be born with special gifts but they can spend their lives studying the dark arts in order to discover more. Knowledge is power, as every true magician knows.

Learn the tricks of the trade from the experts throughout the ages and you, too, could assume the magic mantle. Discover the significance of the magic wand; create your own sacred space; armor yourself against evil; above all, respect the power of focused human thought.

A spell can be whispered or chanted in order to work; it can be written down in familiar words or couched in a secret language; a spell can be worn or even eaten. It may be harnessed to the might of a magic potion or empowered by a single gesture. Cast your spell correctly and it will find its mark.

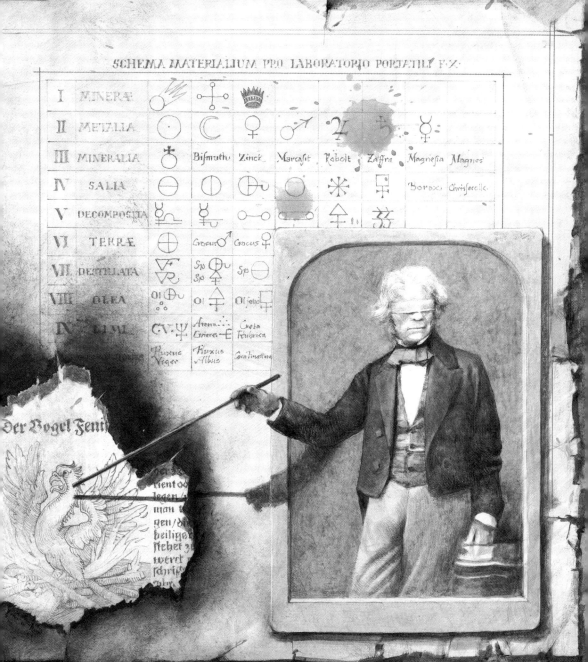

SCHEMA MATERIALIUM PRO LABORATORIO PORTATILI F.Z.

I	MINERÆ								
II	METALLA								
III	MINERALIA		Bismuth	Zinck	Marcasit	Kobolt	Zaffra	Magnesia	Magnes
IV	SALIA							Borax	Chrisocolla
V	DECOMPOSITA								
VI	TERRÆ		Crocus ♂	Crocus ♀					
VII	DESTILLATA		Sp	Sp					
VIII	OLEA		Ol	Ol sabol					
IX	LIMI		Arena Grieres	Creta Rubrica					
		Fluxus Niger	Fluxus Albus	Sal Tintaltus					

Der Vogel Fenir

...rien oo
legen ...
man te
gen / ...
heiliger
stehet zu
werd
schrift
...ber...

THE SORCERER'S APPRENTICE

Making magic requires access to special knowledge hidden from most mortals. Initiation into the mysteries of magic is essential in order to become a successful spell-monger and the training is generally long and arduous. A wizard's studies often include becoming a master of many different branches of science, in addition to immersing oneself in books of magic.

The wisdom sought by a would-be wizard can be imparted by those already in the know. Spell 261 of the ancient Egyptian "Coffin Texts" describes how to become a magician: the chosen one must first address the magicians who are in the presence of the Master of the Universe. He is stripped of his ego to allow the cosmos to penetrate his being and magically empower him. Once initiated, the ancient Egyptian wizard is then permitted to study in the libraries of magic.

To become a shaman—an equally ancient type of wizard with the power to heal and to read the future—a man or woman had not only to possess psychic gifts but also to complete a long training before initiation. A period of fasting was required as part of the initiation rite, in which the shaman "died" and entered the Otherworld, where contact was established with the guardian spirit that would be the source of his or her future powers. The guardian spirit, known as a totem, usually represented an animal, bird, or insect that acted as the shaman's personal protector, guide, and teacher.

There are several other ways in which someone possessing psychic powers could learn the magic arts; one of the most popular was through being apprenticed to a fully fledged wizard. Walt Disney's animated classic "Fantasia" includes the famous "Sorcerer's Apprentice" sequence, starring Mickey Mouse, which is based on an original story dating back to ancient Egyptian times.

In this rendering of the tale, the foolish apprentice decides to cast a spell in his master's absence and animates a broom to fetch water from the well for him. He realizes too late that he doesn't know how to stop it. The

apprentice cuts the broom in two in the hope of breaking the spell, but the broom simply works twice as quickly and the castle is over-flowing with water when the wizard returns. The moral of this tale is that a little knowledge can be a dangerous thing.

Gaining entry into magical places of learning can be a test in itself, as Ged, the hero of "A Wizard of Earthsea" by twentieth-century American author Ursula

Le Guin, discovers. Ged attempts to open the door to the school for wizards on the island of Roke, but is informed by the gatekeeper that it is charmed and will grant access only to someone who can answer its riddle correctly. Fortunately, Ged has the right answer and is allowed to pass through.

Much of the appeal of the "Harry Potter" books lies in Harry's gradual initiation into the complex art of magic at Hogwarts School of Witchcraft and Wizardry, a supernatural boarding school presided over by Professor Dumbledore. At Hogwarts anything is possible, as Harry is taught at his very first lesson by the sinister potions master Severus Snape, who boasts that he can teach how to brew a spell to defy death itself.

MERLIN THE MIGHTY

"Merlin made enchantment
And cast great damage
Into the pavilions, wild fire
That burned bright as a candle clear…"

*A*s far back as this anonymous thirteenth-century English poem and further, Merlin has been revered as a mighty wizard of infinite wisdom and power. He is best known as the great magician of Arthurian legend, who raised Arthur in secret to become king and granted him the enchanted sword Excalibur, whose edge never blunted and whose scabbard could stop bleeding.

Legend has it that Merlin was a magical being, whose mother was a nun and whose father was a demon. The wizard inherited his magic powers and the ability to shape-shift from his father, but his mother instilled in him a love of the mortal world and a desire to help mankind. Although shrouded in myth, Merlin may actually have existed. Some say he was Myrddin, a prophet consulted by royalty, who lived in the Lowlands of Scotland at the end of the sixth century.

In one of the most famous legends about the wizard, Merlin used his magic powers to bring great stones from Ireland to Salisbury Plain for the building of Stonehenge. According to the twelfth-century author Geoffrey of Monmouth in his "History of the Kings of Britain," which laid the foundations of the Arthurian legends, the wizard accompanied a huge British army to accomplish this Herculean feat, but despite their best efforts the 15,000 men were unable to shift the mighty standing stones, known locally as the Giant's Dance:

"Merlin laughed at their vain endeavours … and took down the stones more easily than one could credit and directed their embarkment on board the ships; and so they set sail joyfully back to Britain."

Merlin's ability to divine the future was celebrated by the sixteenth-century English poet Edmund Spenser in "The Faerie Queene," in which the wizard issued prophesies from a Welsh grotto, still known as Merlin's Cave. "Merlin" pamphlets predicting future events were still circulating well into the nineteenth century, such was his popularity.

The English author T. H. White revived and renewed Merlin's powers in his popular story "The Sword in the Stone," published in 1938 and subsequently animated by Walt Disney. As T. H. White explained, the wizard could de-materialize at will. He takes his leave in the book in typical style: "He stood on his toes, while Archimedes held tight to his shoulder: began to spin on them slowly like a top: spun faster and faster till he was only a blur of greyish light: and in a few seconds there was no one there at all."

The most compelling portrait of the great magician was painted by the English author Tolkien, in the guise of the wizard Gandalf, in the trilogy "The Lord of the Rings."

Merlin possessed a fatal weakness. According to certain legends, his lustful nature caused him to be imprisoned by several femmes fatales. It is said that the Lady of the Lake entangled Merlin in a thorn bush by means of spells, and there he remains.

MERLIN

WICKED WORDS

A magic spell may be either written or spoken. Its power lies in the form of the words used—they could be from the wizard's own language—and the way in which they are expressed.

Some of the oldest spells are magical words or phrases, written on parchment and worn around the neck. In the Middle Ages it was commonly believed that the single word "abracadabra" could ward off the Plague, if it was written down and worn around the neck for nine days, then tossed backward over the shoulder into a stream of water flowing eastward. The word is believed to have originated from the ancient Aramaic phrase "abhadda kedhabhra," which meant "disappear like this word." The twentieth-century British wizard Aleister Crowley believed it was a word of great power and that its true form was "abrahadabra." Nowadays, though, it is best known as the prelude to a magic trick performed by a conjuror on stage.

Wizards sometimes used Christian prayers, spoken or written in Latin, or fragments of Christian prayers, as healing spells. The practice was condemned as heresy by the Church and was instrumental in triggering the medieval witch-hunts. An advertisement by a seventeenth-century English wizard promoted a counter-spell against witches, which involved reciting five Paternosters, five Aves and one Credo.

ABRACADABRA
BRACADABR
RACADAB
ACADA
CAD
A

Counter-spells to break evil curses cast by witches were much in demand from customers served by the country-based wizards known as "the cunning ones." It was commonly believed that the magical link that the witch had created with her victim could be used in reverse to punish the witch. The following verse is a nineteenth-century counter-spell against witchcraft:

"He who forges images, he who bewitches
the malevolent aspect, the evil eye,
the malevolent lip, the finest sorcery,
Spirit of the heaven, conjure it!
Spirit of the earth conjure it!"

According to legend, however, leading members of the Church sometimes used counter-spells themselves to ward off wizardry. Apparently, when Druid magicians tried to poison Saint Patrick's drink, he cast the following protective spell over it:

"Tubus fis fri ibu, fis ibu anfis,
Fris bru uatha, ibu lithu, Christi Jesus."

Wizards' spells were used for good or for evil and their power was legion. Spells of transformation were believed to have been able to change lead into gold, or to turn a man into a beast. Spells of invocation could summon spirits out of thin air to do a wizard's bidding. Spells of evocation could influence the heart's desire or even stop time itself. Spells could be cast to manipulate the physical world, to move objects at will, or to make the self invisible. Spells were a way of seeing into the future and a means of solving the world's greatest mysteries.

SONGS OF ENCHANTMENT

The rhythmic or melodic sound of a spell is a powerful element of its magic. It was believed that the rhythmic repetition of a certain word could raise tremendous psychic power that would work the spell.

Power songs were customarily used by shamans to summon their individual guardian spirits. One onlooker provided this vivid nineteenth-century account of a Siberian shaman successfully calling up his animal spirits:

"The beating of the drum grew stronger and stronger, and his song—in which could be heard sounds imitating the howling of the wolf, the groaning of the cargoose, and the voices of the other animals, his guardian spirits—appeared to come, sometimes from the corner nearest my seat, then from the opposite end, then again from the middle of the house, and then it seemed to proceed from the ceiling."

Ritual chanting was a powerful means of spell-casting. The Navaho Indians employed ceremonial chants as healing spells, and these could last for many days and nights. Woe betide the practitioner if they did not chant the spell correctly, though: if they were not word perfect, they could be struck down by the very illness they were seeking to cure.

Today's would-be wizards are advised to use chants to work magic. "The Complete Idiot's Guide to Wicca and Witchcraft" advises: "Within ritual, you can use chants to build your cone of power. Just the way you would with drumming, you start out slow; then you build the pace and raise the volume. You chant faster and louder until you feel ready to burst with the energy. But don't pop. Direct the energy you've raised into your magick tool or object."

This contemporary magical chant is used by wizards to build a rhythmic momentum through repetition, in the manner of drumming, in order to induce a trance-like state to empower an act of magic.

"Eko Eko Azarak

Eko Eko Zomelak

Eko Eko Cerunnos

Eko Eko Aradia."

In ancient times, wizards believed that the sound vibrations caused when speaking the secret names of God during magic rituals could unleash an incredible cosmic force. So powerful was the personal name of God in the Old Testament that wizards could only whisper it.

While speaking certain names of power was forbidden unless they were needed for the most powerful magic, most spells had to be uttered forcefully to be effective. The female wizards of ancient Greece were said to howl their magical chants and the legendary Sirens of Greek mythology used enchanted songs to bind men to their will. The ancient Greek theologian Clement of Alexandria warned all men to beware of Siren magic: "Sail past the song; it works death; exert your will, and you have overcome ruin; bound to the wood of the Cross, you shall be freed from destruction."

The power of song, according to folk tradition, was harnessed very effectively by the siren-like mermaids, who lured mortal men to a watery grave and feasted on their souls. The potency of their song was described by Shakespeare's fairy King Oberon:

"The rude sea grew civil at her song
And certain stars shot madly from their spheres
To hear the sea-maid's music."

DOCTOR DEE AND ANGEL MAGIC

*T*he last royal magician, John Dee was astrologer to Queen Elizabeth I and a powerful figure at the English court. A gifted mathematician and map-maker, Dee was known as the most learned man in Europe at the time, but his lifelong fascination with astrology, alchemy, and angel magic made him widely feared as a powerful wizard.

Doctor Dee amassed a great library of books on magic and the occult, and turned a wing of his London house into a laboratory where he conducted alchemical experiments. To discover the secret of transmuting base metals into gold, however, he needed to communicate with angels. It is said that with the help of a fellow alchemist, Edward Kelley, who acted as a medium, Dee possessed sufficient magical power to summon angels and to discover an elixir of trans-mutation. Records of Dee's angelic conversations were published shortly after his death in 1608, in an extraordinary book entitled "A True and Faithful Relation of What Passed for Many Years Between Dr John Dee and Some Spirits."

The first successful summoning apparently occurred at his home just before Christmas in 1581, when Dee conjured the angel Anael. A few months later, Dee found himself conversing with the archangel Uriel, who presented the doctor with a new crystal ball and also gave instructions for the layout of the "holy table" and the "seal of god" to help him with his alchemy. According to Dee, Uriel appeared floating outside his window, holding a pale-pink crystal about the size of an orange. They were joined by the archangel Michael, who told Dee that the crystal could be used to summon other angels.

This crystal, which Kelley successfully used to summon spirits so that Dee could converse with them, is on display at the British Museum in London. Kelley would gaze into the magic "shew stone" and call to the angels to appear before Dee. The angels then taught the two men a special system of magic, now known as Enochian, which could be used to make a spirit carry out a wizard's spell.

The angelic séances ended after a young female spirit-guide, Madimi, appeared naked and encouraged the two men to indulge in wife-swapping. Both wives objected, quarrels broke out and the two associates parted company. Dee lives on as the inspiration of the imperious wizard Prospero in Shakespeare's play "The Tempest," who summons the spirit Ariel to do his bidding, or else:

"I will rend an oak
And peg thee in his knotty entrails till
Thou hast howl'd away twelve winters."

JOHN DEE

A CHARMED LIFE

A wizard's spell worn next to the skin was considered to be a powerful magic charm. It could take the form of a protective amulet to ward off illness or danger, or it might be an enchanted talisman to attract health and good fortune. Such charms were all-important in ancient Egypt. The following instructions, from the "Leyden Magical Papyrus," explain how to create the ultimate talisman:

"Take a linen band with sixteen threads (four white, four green, four blue, four red), dye them with the blood of a hoopoe and tie them to a scarab in the form of the Sun god clothed in the finest linen."

The practice of creating a figurine image of the subject of a spell probably originated with the shabti figures created by the wizards of ancient Egypt. Such likenesses, subsequently known as "poppets," were believed to contain the living essence of the person they were made to resemble. If the spell was a curse, the poppet would be tortured, but poppets could also be fashioned for beneficial magic.

Stones have long been credited with inherent magical powers, particularly if they are round, or have a hole. Certain round stones in Ireland are known as "cursing stones" because turning them clockwise during a spell can cast an ill-luck charm on someone. The seventeenth-century Scottish wizard Coinneach Odhar is believed to have been granted the power of divination with the help of a stone with a hole in it that appeared magically on his chest while he lay sleeping in a field.

Wearing or carrying charms could enhance a wizard's powers because they protected the wearer from negative energy; in order to function properly, however, they must first be charged with magic. Often such charms were worn as rings. According to legend, King Solomon had a magic ring etched with a hexagram and the secret name of God, which enabled him to summon demons to do his bidding.

The ultimate magic ring was the powerful talisman at the centre of the battle between good and evil in Tolkien's trilogy "The Lord of the Rings." Cool to the touch, although it had been plucked from the heart of a fire, the ring reveals the fiery rune inscription "One Ring to rule them all, One Ring to find them, One Ring to bring them all and in the darkness bind them." Like Tolkien, the nineteenth-century composer Wagner created his great cycle of operas "Der Ring des Nibelungen" around a magic ring of power:

"A shaft of light from the heavens suddenly illuminates the Rhine treasure, the priceless hoard of gold.... The gold may be forged into a Ring which will allow its owner to rule the World. Alberich wrenches the treasure from its hiding place. he forges the Ring of Power. Everyone is threatened, even the gods themselves."

THE WIZARD'S WAND

A king or queen bears a scepter as a potent symbol of royalty; the wizard's scepter of power is his magic staff. In this case, though, it is much more than just a symbol—it is the concentrated focus of the wizard's magic. The mightier the wizard, the more awesome the power of their wand as a force for good or evil.

One of the earliest and most impressive magic wands was made for Jupiter, the supreme god of Classical mythology, who was worshiped as lord of the heavens and bringer of light. His scepter was forged by the god Vulcan, who created thunderbolts. The wizard-god Mercury used a wand with two serpents entwined upon it to conduct spirits to the Underworld. With his "opiate rod," as it was described by the seventeenth-century English poet John Milton, Mercury could cast spells of enchanted sleep among other magical procedures.

Archaeologists believe they may have discovered the earliest-known British wizard, during the excavation of a ceremonial burial site in South Wales, dating from around 24,000 BC. In the Paviland Tomb, they found the corpse of a young man buried with ivory mammoth tusks that had been deliberately broken. Ivory was revered as a magical material at that time and the fact that it had been deliberately broken may indicate that it was a magic scepter that would have been ritually destroyed at the wizard's death.

The deliberate breaking of a wizard's wand may also be carried out in order to put an end to spell-casting, along with the destruction of books of magic, as Shakespeare's wizard Prospero shows in "The Tempest":

"Graves at my command
have wak'd their sleepers, op'd, and let 'em forth,
By my potent art. But this rough magic
I here abjure …
I'll break my staff,
Bury it certain fathoms in the earth,
And deeper than ever did plummet sound
I'll drown my book."

All-powerful Jupiter, one of the earliest and greatest wand-wielders, was worshiped as the bringer of light, and the wizard's staff is traditionally revered for using powerful magic to illuminate the darkness and thus, symbolically, to overcome evil. The shocking transformation of a wooden stick into the ultimate magic weapon in a desperate duel between the young wizard Ged and the evil shadow-beast, is vividly described by Ursula Le Guin in her book "A Wizard of Earthsea":

"Ged lifted up the staff high, and the radiance of it brightened intolerably, burning with so white and great a light that it compelled and harrowed even that ancient darkness. In that light all form of man sloughed off the thing that came towards Ged. It drew together and shrank and blackened."

ODIN, MASTER OF THE RUNES

*T*he greatest of the Norse gods, Odin was worshiped as "All-Father" and possessed magical powers of such magnitude that he was even able to discover the wisdom of the Runes, the secret alphabetical key to life itself. This was a miraculous feat and Odin paid dearly to achieve it. He pierced himself with his magical spear Gungnir, which had been forged by dwarves, and hung as a sacrificed corpse from the World Tree for nine days and nine nights. At the end of that dreadful time Odin received his reward, as he uttered these words:

"I peered downward,
I grasped the Runes,
Screeching I grasped them."

Possession of these magical alphabetical characters enabled Odin to access secret wisdom dating back to the creation of the world. Odin passed on this precious knowledge to both gods and men. Runic letters have since been used in divination, magic, and meditation. It is said that when Runic characters are combined as "Bind Runes," they create a magical talisman of great protective power.

Empowered by such superior wisdom, Odin became the Lord of the Gallows and a master of ghosts. He was able to carve and color the Runes, thus bringing corpses back to life, which then spoke to him, revealing occult secrets of the dead.

Mounted on his magical eight-legged steed Sleipnir, Odin galloped over the sea and through the sky. Master of the Universe, he journeyed beyond death and rode into the Underworld in order to consult its resident prophetess about the nature of his son Balder's death. The prophetess penetrated Odin's disguise, however, and refused to answer all his questions.

Others were less successful in recognizing Odin who, as supreme shape-shifter, was a master of disguise. In order to drink the closely guarded heavenly Mead of Poetry and acquire great magical wisdom, the Norse wizard transformed himself first into a giant and labored as a field hand for Baugi, the brother of Suttung to whom the mead had been entrusted. He worked with super-human strength in the hope that he would be rewarded with a sip. When that attempt failed, he shifted into a serpent and slithered through a tiny hole he had drilled into the mountain cavern where the secret brew was kept. There, he changed into a handsome youth with whom the solitary female guard fell so deeply in love that she allowed him to drain the well to its dregs, after which Odin transformed into an eagle and flew away to safety.

Like many great wizards, Odin possessed a fabulous golden ring. Forged by two dwarves, it produced eight further magic rings every ninth night. More unusually, he wore this ring around his arm, rather than on his finger. Odin lives on as Wotan in the nineteenth-century German composer Richard Wagner's operatic cycle "The Ring of the Nibelung."

ODIN

BREWS AND STEWS

drunk instead by a youth named Gwydion, a humble servant put in charge of stirring the cauldron.

Instantly empowered, Gwydion fled from the angry goddess by shape-shifting into a hare, a fish, an otter, and a bird, but she caught up with him and pounced and ate him when he changed into a single grain of wheat among a multitude in a desperate attempt to elude her.

Once inside Cerridwen's stomach, he transformed again, this time into an unborn child. The goddess gave birth to a baby son of radiant beauty nine months later, who grew up to become the great Welsh bard and prophet Taliesin. He used his songs and music to work all kinds of wonders, and could travel through time and space, shape-shift and calm storms with a single word. His gifts were due to his miraculous conception, as the sixth-century "Book of Taliesin" records:

"Gwydion created me, great magic from
the staff of enchantment …
From five fifties of magicians and teachers
Like Math was I produced …
The magician of magicians created
Me before the world."

The cauldron has been the tool of witches and wizards from time immemorial. In the earliest beliefs, it was associated with fertility of such concentrated power it could even revive the dead.

A magic cauldron, according to legend, was instrumental in the making of the legendary Welsh wizard Taliesin. Its enchanted brew had been boiled for a year and a day by the Celtic goddess of magic Cerridwen to yield three drops of knowledge, inspiration, and science for her ugly son Avaggdu. But the drops were

The best-known magic cauldron, however, is the one stirred by Shakespeare's three witches in "Macbeth," into which they memorably drop:

> "Eye of newt, and toe of frog,
> Wool of bat, and tongue of dog,
> Adder's fork, and blind-worm's sting,
> Lizard's leg, and howlet's wing,
> For a charm of powerful trouble,
> Like a hell-broth boil and bubble."

Magic-making shifted to the laboratory when wizards began to pursue the science of alchemy, and the cauldron was replaced by an elaborate assortment of apparatus needed to conduct the necessary experiments. An early Greek vessel used to vaporize acidic liquids that would attack metals, took the form of a tube with a furnace at the bottom and a condensing dome at the top. Another key item was a crucible and an aludel, a pear-shaped glass or earthenware pot used for sublimation.

Folk legend provides this atmospheric description of the sixteenth-century laboratory of the Irish wizard earl, Gerald Fitzgerald:

"It was a strange, old high-vaulted room, set about with magical implements and great stoppered jars which seemed to bubble and hiss with mysterious contents. There were large casks, too, which appeared to contain the dust of human bodies, and glass bottles in which floated preserved anatomical parts, both human and animal. In a shadowy corner stood the great mirror in which visions of distant parts of the world came and went. The whole place fairly seethed of ancient magic."

THE MAGIC MANTLE

It has often been observed that "the clothes make the man" and this is particularly true for would-be wizards, as demonstrated by a twenty-first-century handbook on Wicca, which gives the following advice for apprentice magicians:

"Your magickal clothing is another way you can add power to your magick. When you wear your magickal clothing it lets the subconscious know that there is work to be done. Your magickal clothing can also carry magickal symbols or messages. This too will help empower the clothing."

This was the style of dress favored by Merlyn in T. H. White's book "The Sword in the Stone." His exotic attire is described in great detail and it conjures up an archetypal image of a wizard:

"He was dressed in a flowing gown with fur tippets which had the signs of the zodiac embroidered all over it, together with various cabalistic signs, as of triangles with eyes in them, queer crosses, leaves of trees, bones and birds and animals and a planetarium whose stars shone like bits of looking glass with the sun on them. he had a pointed hat like a dunce's cap.... he also had a wand of lignum vitae … and a pair of horn-rimmed spectacles."

As befits the kings or queens of their craft, the robes worn by ancient wizards were similarly majestic—albeit in an occult way. The later addition of a pointed hat gave the wizard a more towering majesty, while the spectacles lent him a more scholarly aspect. The ritual vestment worn by the arch-magicians of ancient Egypt was a tawny skin spangled with stars, later copied in the celestial cloaks traditionally worn by French kings at their coronations.

The shaman was equipped with a special costume to help him on his journey into the spirit world. It was highly elaborate with many objects embroidered on or hanging from it to symbolize the various creatures he would use as guides. A shaman often donned a bird-cloak made of feathers to represent his transformation into a bird-soul during his ecstatic trance. Such a garment is described in the ninth-century Irish "Glossary of Cormac." The fantastic cloak was "made of the skins of white and many-colored birds; up to his girdle of the necks of mallards, and from his girdle up to his neck of their tufts."

Wizards may traditionally wear such impressive clothing when practicing ritual magic in private. However, when traveling, they customarily dress down in order to appear less conspicuous. This is most famously illustrated by Tolkien's fictional wizard Gandalf. He is first introduced to the reader when he enters the Shire—the domain of the Hobbits—as an old man wearing a tall pointed blue hat, a long grey cloak, and a silver scarf. When the time is right, however, Gandalf is revealed in his true colors.

Gandalf drew on mighty magic to defeat the monstrous Balrog and, in the process, transformed himself from Galdalf the Grey into Gandalf the White. He stands revealed as a more powerful magician than the evil wizard Saruman the White, whose own former radiance is now clouded by evil.

ESSENTIAL AIDS

Successful spell-casting may require specific tools, quite apart from a magic wand or a bubbling cauldron.

A well-stocked library is a necessity for wizards pursuing elaborate ritual magic or alchemy. The Tudor court magician Doctor John Dee had a magnificent library, comprising over 4,000 volumes, but it was ransacked and largely destroyed by an angry mob intent on punishing the man they feared as an evil sorcerer.

Some of the most ancient handbooks of magic are known as "black books" or "grimoires." These began to circulate in the Middle Ages and newer versions are still consulted by students of ceremonial magic. These volumes offer precise instructions for various rituals and advice on how to conjure and control demons. The greatest "black book" is "The Key of Solomon," which has provided material for many others and is attributed to King Solomon, the general of a demonic army.

Candles have also played a major role in magical ceremonies for many centuries. Ancient Egyptian magicians used candlelight for divination, and the practice continues to the present day. One procedure practiced in ancient Egypt required the wizard to write specific hieroglyphs and symbols on a clean wick in a new lamp. The lamp was set upon a brick and the wizard would cast a spell to conjure a spirit who would be attracted to the flame; he could then question the spirit about magical matters. The magic lamp immortalized in the story of Aladdin, which could summon a powerful genie, derives from such early divination ceremonies.

Candles made of human fat were believed by some to contain life energy and were used in black-magic rituals. Whatever the occasion, it has always been vital to use the correct candle for the work in hand. A modern Wicca spell to lose weight requires a black candle on which the magician must write the weight loss desired. As it burns, the following spell is chanted:

> "As this candle melts away,
> So do the pounds that hold me sway.
> As each day passes I will be
> Closer to a thinner me.
> This is my will, so mote it be!"

Runes could be cast to invoke spirits or divine the future. The Roman author Tacitus described in AD 98 how the Germanic people threw rune staves on to a white cloth for divinatory purposes. They were then interpreted by a rune master or rune mistress. A thirteenth-century rune mistress could easily have been mistaken for one of today's wizards, as this contemporary description shows:

"She wore a cloak set with stones along the hem. Around her neck and covering her head she wore a hood lined with white cat skins. In one hand she carried a staff with a knob on the end and on her belt, holding together her long dress, hung a charm pouch."

Tarot cards can also be used by adepts as a magical means of foretelling the future. They were thought by some wizards to contain the lost magical wisdom of the Egyptian god Thoth. Others believed that by learning Tarot wisdom, a practitioner could step off the wheel of fate and control his or her destiny. The nineteenth-century British wizard Arthur Edward Waite and fellow members of the magical Order of the Golden Dawn, associated the four suits in a pack of cards with the four sacred objects of the Holy Grail quest: pentacles, cups, wands, and swords.

CRYSTAL CLEAR

The arch-magicians of ancient Egypt used quartz-crystal balls to concentrate the rays of the Sun on a patient when casting their healing spells. The stone is still associated with magical healing powers, largely due to the widespread belief that it possesses a high level of natural energy that can be released by adepts to empower others. This theory gained more credence following the discovery by the twentieth-century Russian scientist Semyon Kirlian that crystals were surrounded by radiating energy fields.

Wizards throughout the ages have also employed the crystal ball to see into the future. This method of divination became popular in Europe in the fifteenth century, when it was popularly believed that magicians could conjure spirits or angels to appear in the glass and carry out their bidding.

The sixteenth-century wizard John Dee famously possessed such a magic ball, which he used with the medium Edward Kelley to summon angels. He recorded that it was presented to him by the angel Uriel. Doctor Dee also employed a magic mirror made of polished black obsidian, reportedly taken from Mexico by the Spanish explorer Hernán Cortés.

The magic mirror has also been used as a method of divination since time immemorial. Mirrors have always had a special significance in magic. They are still believed by some to reflect the soul and must thus be carefully guarded lest the soul be lost. Magicians would stare into the reflective surface of a mirror until they hypnotized themselves into a mystic trance, in which they could communicate with visionary beings.

The medieval magician Albertus Magnus provided the following instructions for making a magic mirror, but he included a warning that a dog or a cat should be used to test it first:

"Buy a looking glass and inscribe upon it 'S. Solam. S. Tattler. S. Echogordner Gematur.' Bury it at a crossroads during an uneven hour. On the third day, go to the spot at the same hour and dig it up—but do not be the first person to gaze into it."

The magic power of the mirror has been much celebrated in fiction. Snow White's sorceress stepmother memorably consults one, while Lewis Carroll's Alice famously steps through a looking glass on her magical journey into Wonderland. It is a magic mirror, too, that empowers Harry Potter to reach the Philosopher's Stone, rather than losing it to the evil wizard Voldemort in their desperate battle of wits in J. K. Rowling's story of the same name.

A still pool of water can also be used to powerful magical effect, as Frodo, the hero of Tolkien's "The Lord of the Rings," discovers when he is invited to use the Mirror of Galadriel and is nearly ensnared by the arch-wizard Sauron.

"Magick mirror before my eyes,
See my needs and hear my cries.
Ring out the beauty that lies within,
Start the spell let the magick begin.
Through this glass my reflection I see,
My intent, my will, so mote it be!"

safety of a magic circle; however, the protective magic would only work if she remained silent:

"'Stand where you are!' commanded the Earl, and he drew a chalk circle all around her. To this he added inexplicable glyphs and signs, so that in the end, his wife stood in the middle of a curious pentagram. 'Now,' he said. 'As long as you stay where you are and make no sound, in spite of what you see, nothing will harm you. But if you should move or utter even the smallest noise there will be dire consequences for us all.'"

When she screamed at the monsters he conjured, they all sank forever under the waters of the lake.

A magic circle should ideally be cast with a consecrated dagger, sword, or wand, during the correct astrological conditions and at a designated time of the day or night. According to magic tradition, the circle should be nine feet in diameter, or a double circle comprising a smaller circle with a diameter of eight feet, within a larger one of ten feet. When casting a circle, a wizard should move clockwise to echo the motion of the Universe. In black-magic rituals, however, a wizard moves counterclockwise, thus reversing the norm and unleashing negative energy.

Wizards can strengthen the magical power of the circle by inscribing specific symbols within it. One of the most potent is the pentacle, a five-pointed star in a circle within a circle, which symbolizes divine power. This was often deployed as a defence against demons, as illustrated in the Italian poet Ludovico Ariosto's sixteenth-century epic "Orlando Furioso":

"And on her head, lest spirits should invade,
A pentacle, for more assurance, laid."

*P*owerful spells can be cast within a sacred space and the most potent sacred space is the magic circle.

The circle symbolizes wholeness and unity. For wizards, it can provide a boundary for a reservoir of concentrated energy and a doorway to the world of spirits. Woe betide those who step outside the protective boundary of the magic circle, however, lest a conjured evil spirit grabs them, or the spell goes badly wrong.

A dramatic example of what could happen if the spell is broken is described in the legend of the sixteenth-century wizard Earl Desmond. He made the mistake of permitting his wife to watch his powerful spell-casting from the

MICHAEL SCOT AND HIS MAGIC TRAVELS

*L*egend has it that it was Michael Scot's forbidden tasting of the magical fish of knowledge that transformed him from a man into a wizard. Warned to watch but not touch as the fish cooked, he had burned his fingers on its enchanted flesh, cooled them in his mouth—and in this way he received his first potent taste of magic. After that there was no turning back. Already respected as a mathematician, physician, and astrologer, the thirteenth-century Scottish nobleman and scholar was soon revered as a magician possessing great supernatural powers.

There were apparently no limits to Scot's abilities. It was said he had summoned the Devil to help him build a road in Scotland in a single night and that he could make the bells of Notre Dame in Paris peal out with a wave of his wand. Perhaps Scot could even transform base metal into gold. He certainly dabbled in alchemy and recommended the following arcane concoction to perform the ultimate magical feat: "Mix the blood of a ruddy man and the blood of a red owl with saffron, alum, urine, and cucumber juice."

Magical mounts that galloped at the speed of thought carried Scot wherever he desired to go. He rode through the air on a fairy horse and sailed the oceans on the back of a fantastical sea creature.

Scot's most famous journey was a whirlwind aerial ride from Scotland to Rome on the back of a witch, for an audience with the Pope. Before the Pope would agree to see him, however, Scot had to prove that he had come from Scotland. Scot told him that he had ridden so swiftly that he still had the snow of his native country on his bonnet.

"What proof," asked the Pope, "can you give me of that?"

"That a shoe on your foot is not your own," Scot replied.

The Pope looked down, and on his right foot was a woman's shoe. "You will get what you want," he said to Scot, "and begone."

Scot was rewarded by learning a vital secret that the Pope kept to himself—that the first Tuesday of the first Moon of spring was shrove-tide.

The Scot was immortalized by the fourteenth-century Italian poet Dante in "The Divine Comedy," in which he placed the wizard in the eighth circle of the Inferno.

Scot is believed to have been buried in Melrose Abbey in Scotland. It is said that a "wondrous light" burns eternally within his tomb to ward off evil spirits.

MICHAEL SCOT

PART III

⭐

SPELLS FOR DIFFERENT PURPOSES

*W*hat if we could make our dreams come true? Deepest love, radiant health, limitless wealth, endless power—could we really achieve all, or even one, of these things?

Mighty wizards of the past have certainly claimed that it was within their powers to work such wonders. Better still, they have passed down to us many of the actual spells they cast. Modern wizards are equally convinced. They, too, believe that they possess the necessary magic to change lives. Together they have created a vast body of magic. Could some of their spells work for you?

8	3	4
	5	9
	7	2

Atropa *Belladonna*

Viscum album

Bubble, bubble, toil, and trouble,
Strengthen this potion on the double.
Empower this magik, send it fast,
And it harm none, make it last.

A
G
L A

A
B
C
D
E
F
G
H
I
J
K
L
M
N
O
P
Q
R
S
T
U
V
W
X
Y
Z

SWEET DREAMS

Dreams can be the doorway to another world. The arch-magicians of ancient Egypt used candles to "dream true": by sitting in a south-facing cave in darkness and gazing into the candle flame, a wizard might enter a dream-like trance and call upon a deity to grant his desires.

A twentieth-dynasty Egyptian spell describes how a man should address the summoned god while in a dream trance, in order to persuade a particular woman to love him. The threat included at the end due to his desperation, however, may not have gone down very well:

"Hail to thee, O Re-harakhte,
Father of the Gods!
hail to you,
O ye Seven hathors
Who are adorned
With strings of red thread!
hail to you, ye Gods
Lords of heaven and earth!
Come make [Insert chosen name]
Born of [Insert names of father and mother of chosen person] come after me,
Like an ox after grass,
Like a servant after her children
Like a drover after his herd.

If you do not make her come after me,
Then I will set fire to Busiris
And burn up Osiris."

Lovers throughout the ages have used magical dream-spells to identify a future lover. Pillow magic can be an effective way of achieving this. A traditional spell to discover the identity of your future husband is to place a prayer book opened at the marriage service under your pillow on a Wednesday or a Saturday night. In order to ensure that your bridegroom comes to you in your dream, the book should be open at the page that says "With this ring I thee wed" and it must be bound with a scarlet-and-white ribbon and bear a sprig of myrtle.

Magical dreams to conjure future husbands can go badly wrong, however. A nineteenth-century Scottish legend records the cautionary tale of a young woman who successfully summoned her lover in her dreams by means of a complicated spell involving holly leaves and three pails of water. While with her, however, he "let fall a rope with a noose at the end, which the young woman took up the next morning and laid in her press." The couple were married soon after, but less than a fortnight after the wedding, the groom hanged himself with the rope.

FATA MORGANA, WICKED ENCHANTRESS

"For all her looks were full of spells,
And all her words, of sorcery;
And in some way they seemed to say,
'Oh, come with me!'"

Mortal men were powerless to resist the fatal allure of the beautiful wizard Morgana—also known as Morgan Le Fay—as the nineteenth-century British poet Madison Cawein makes chillingly clear in this poem. In it he describes the night the wily "Queen of Shadowland" led King Arthur's knight Sir Kay to a hideous death by "the hundred blades."

To a large extent, Fata Morgana—the ultimate femme fatale—was the invention of medieval romance writers such as Sir Thomas Malory, who immortalized her in his fifteenth-century epic "Le Morte D'Arthur" as a wicked enchantress constantly bent on the king's death. She plotted to steal Arthur's magical sword Excalibur and his throne, but failed in both attempts.

According to Malory, Morgana was the third sister of King Arthur and that, alarmingly, she was initiated into the magic arts during her convent education. She "was put to school in a nunnery," he wrote, "and there she learned so much that she was a great clerk of necromancy."

So powerful were Morgana's charms that she ensnared King Arthur's magical adviser, the wizard Merlin, and made him teach her all he knew. She tricked him into revealing the secret of constructing a tower of air, then imprisoned him inside it.

A notorious shape-shifter, Morgana could transform at will from a beautiful young woman into an ugly old crone. In the English medieval poem "Sir Gawain and the Green Knight," Arthur's knight Sir Gawain finds himself in the castle of a giant. The giant bids the knight sleep with his lovely wife; when she comes to his chamber he refuses her kisses, but accepts a magic girdle that she offers him. This saves Gawain from death when the Green Knight later tries to behead him, but does not prevent him from receiving a bad neck wound. Gawain discovers that his delightful seductress is actually an ancient hag and that both she and the Green Knight are manifestations of Morgan Le Fay, who had hoped to kill him.

Legend has it that Fata Morgana was originally Morrigan, also known as Morrigu, an ancient Irish war goddess with the power to conjure magic fogs and rain. She sometimes appeared on battlefields as a raven eating the bodies of the dead. The terror of encountering her in any of her manifestations is vividly described in the early Irish epic "Tain Bo Cuailnge":

"Over his head is shrieking
A lean hag, quickly hopping
Over the points of the weapons and the shield;
She is grey-haired Morrigu."

MORGANA

LOVE CHARMS

Perhaps the best-known magical love potion is the one used in anger by the fairy King Oberon in Shakespeare's "A Midsummer Night's Dream" in order to humiliate his Queen by making her fall in love with an ass. The elixir was the juice of a flower that had been transformed by Cupid's dart into a strong love potion:

"I'll drop the liquor of it in her eyes;
The next thing then she waking looks upon,
Be it lion, or wolf, or bull,
On meddling monkey, or on busy ape,
She shall pursue it with the soul of love."

Those unable to acquire such a flower in order to win their true love's heart might attempt this elaborate love charm inscribed on an ancient Greek payrus:

"Make a figure of a dog eight fingers long out of wax and gum. Write magical words on the figure where the ribs are. On a separate lead tablet, write the names of the demons who are being called upon to assist. Then place the tablet on a tripod and the dog on the tablet. Recite the words of power written on the side of the dog and the names written on the tablet. If the dog snarls, the spell will not be successful. If it barks, it will be a success."

Less experienced magicians, however, would find this twenty-first-century love charm much simpler:

"Drip water gathered under a full Moon on to a photograph of yourself with your beloved. Visualize your beloved arriving from afar to find you and chant these words:

Sacred water flow from me
To draw him ever near
As endless rivers run to sea
his path to me is clear.

A love that's true once here he'll find
And know his journey's end.
And in his heart and soul and mind
he'll know our lives should blend.'"

Flower magic can be used to similar effect, as in this traditional love charm—although it is probably best employed under cover of darkness by those who fall for the boy or girl next door, to avoid social embarrassment:

"**S**trew five red roses along the pathway between your home and your lover's home, while calling your lover's name. Then, from a sixth rose burn five red petals, one after the other, in the flame of a pure beeswax candle, while chanting:

Burn a pathway to my door, five rose petals now are four.
Four to three in candle fire, bringing closer my desire
Three to two, I burn the rose, love no hesitation shows
Burn two to one, till there are none, the spell is done
Come lover, come.'"

FRUITS OF DESIRE

The quest for the most effective love spell has preoccupied wizards for many centuries. A key ingredient of the most favored magical procedures is the apple, a fruit long associated with love and marriage. This traditional spell to attract your true love requires the most perfect example you can find:

"On Friday early as may be,
Take the fairest apple from the tree,
Then in thy blood on paper white
Thine own name and thy true love's write.
That apple thou shalt cut in two
And for its cure that paper put,
With two sharp pins or myrtle wood
Join the halves till it seem good,
In the oven let it dry:
And wrapped in the leaves of myrtle lie,
Under the pillow of thy dear,
Yet let it be unknown to her.
And if it a secret be
She soon will show her love for thee."

So powerful is apple love magic that all parts of the fruit can be employed to good effect. To discover the identity of a future lover, for example, peel an apple in one long strip at midnight on Hallowe'en and throw it over your left shoulder with your right hand. When it falls to the ground, it will form the initial of their Christian name.

Apple pips could be used to find out where he or she lived, as in this traditional spell from Lancashire, England:

Walk in a circle, squeezing an apple core so hard between the finger and thumb that a pip shoots out, while reciting:

Pippin, pippin, paradise,
Tell me where my true love lies;
East, West, North, or South,
Piling brig or Cocker-mouth."

Mandzagoza

Take care to observe carefully the direction that the flying pip took, for that is the way to your true love's home.

The distinctive mandrake root, often shaped like a grotesque human figure, is popularly known as the "love apple." It has long been revered in magical circles as a powerful aphrodisiac. The ancient Egyptians called mandrake the Phallus of the Field, while Arabs referred to it as the Devil's Testicles.

Acquiring a root was fraught with problems, however. It was reputed to emit such a powerful shriek when pulled out of the ground that it would drive any living thing mad. Early spell-casters were advised to use a starving dog to do the job for them. A shaving of the root boiled up with a single hair was enough to produce a powerful summoning charm.

Mandrake still features in contemporary love spells. American High Priestess of magic Laurie Cabot recommends mandrake root is blended with coriander, yarrow, dragon's blood, and oil in this "Gay Man's" love spell:

"Blend the herbs while envisioning yourselves in a variety of romantic settings. Carve your name on one side of a pink candle and your lover's on the other. Cast a circle. Then envision yourself as lovers while anointing the pink candle. Next, burn the herbal mixture as incense and light a black candle, then the pink candle and a white candle."

Write this spell on parchment and read it out loud while touching the parchment to each candle flame:

"Flame of love, burn strong and bright,
Fill his heart with my loving light,
[state your name and your lover's name]
No other man will he see,
With loving arms he will come to me.
So mote it be."

Let the parchment burn in an ash pot. As the flame rises say, "In correctness and for the good of all." Carry the ashes in a black bag, or hang it on your bedpost, or bury it where it will not be disturbed.

LOOKS COULD KILL

The belief that an enemy could inflict disease or death merely by glancing at his or her victim dates back to some of the earliest civilizations and quick reactions are required if anyone is unfortunate enough to be struck down by the power of the "evil eye."

For the ancient Egyptians, the eye was all-important. The symbol of an eye meant "to create" in Egyptian and it signified wholeness. This was emphasized in this chant, uttered in the final stages of initiation as a magician:

> "I have applied the Eye of horus to you so that your face may be regenerated by it. I have anointed your eyes with the green ointment and the black ointment so that your face may be regenerated by them.... I complete your face with ointment from the Eye of horus, by which it was completed. he reattaches your bones, he reassembles your limbs, he reunites your flesh and scatters your ills."

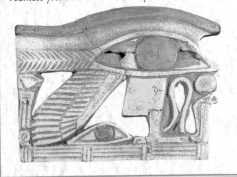

Strong magic was needed by the wizards of ancient Egypt to combat the "evil eye" and a complex magical procedure was devised, known as the "rite of hitting a ball,"

in which the ball signified the evil eye. The spell necessitated the ritual killing of an oryx, a crocodile, and a tortoise.

An armory of magic charms to ward off the "evil eye" has been assembled through the centuries. The best defence, it is said, is to wear an amulet because of the protective magical properties with which it is imbued. Specific hand gestures can also be effective, however, if made quickly enough. An illustrated book of the best hand positions to use was published in 1895, and a popular defence was the "fig" position—a clenched fist with the thumb thrust between the index and middle fingers.

Hand positions to ward off the Evil Eye

Help has always been available for a victim unable to retaliate on the spot. He or she could always cast a counter-spell, such as this twenty-first-century charm:

> "Take a length of silver cord and tie a knot in each end. As you do so, visualize yourself as one knot and the source of evil as the other. Cut the cord in the center with a magick knife and chant these words:
>
> From you to me this spell I break
> This path was not right for you to make
> Its path I will abruptly end,
> And back to you the spell I send.'"

GERALD FITZGERALD, THE WIZARD EARL

*I*t is said that far below the tranquil surface of Lough Guir in Ireland, there still dwells that country's mightiest magician, the sixteenth-century wizard Gerald Fitzgerald, Earl of Desmond.

Earl Desmond's reign as a powerful sorcerer came to an abrupt end one dark and stormy night, when his wife, who was sworn to be silent forever, screamed out as her husband shape-shifted into a hideous giant. The spell was broken and, in an instant, they and their island castle sank down to the bottom of the lake.

Death, apparently, has no dominion over the Wizard Earl. Every seven years, he re-emerges from the deep to haunt the living. At midnight on the anniversary of the sinking of the castle, he steps ashore to seize the unwary and carry them down to his watery home.

A washerwoman named Moll Rail narrowly escaped such a fate in the late-nineteenth century, when she encountered the ghostly Earl while she was out washing clothes in the lake. The wizard tried to abduct her by offering her a ring of gold. Fortunately, Moll was clumsy and as she took the ring, it slipped from her hand and fell with a splash into the lough before she could put it on and fall under his spell.

The fearful respect Earl Desmond commanded following his mysterious disappearance was nothing compared to the abject terror he inspired at the height of his magical powers. The Church accused him of consorting with demons and it was widely believed that he summoned evil spirits to do his bidding from a secret chamber situated in the highest tower of his castle.

Indeed, it was his wife's first-hand experience of the Earl's awesome summoning charms that brought about his downfall. According to folklore, she was cursed with an insatiable curiosity and plagued her husband incessantly about demonstrating his magical arts to her—to the point where he eventually capitulated. He agreed to her request, however, on the binding condition that she should remain silent throughout.

True to his word, the next evening the wizard took his wife to his secret chamber. He told her to stand still and silent and drew a chalk circle around her and within it he drew many occult signs and symbols. He then lit a brazier, cast herbs upon it and downed the contents of a small phial.

As his wife watched, her husband sprouted feathers and became a huge vulture, then transformed into a dwarfish hag, who tried to grab her from outside the circle. Next, the hag shape-shifted into a monstrous serpent that attempted to strike her. Finally, the snake turned back into her husband. But this proved to be the biggest shock of all:

"The Earl laid himself on the floor of the chamber, just outside the outer rim of the chalk circle, and he began to stretch. Longer and longer he grew, his face becoming more misshapen, until his vast head was almost touching one wall of the room and his heels reached the other. His arms and legs had stretched out of all recognition. An intense horror suddenly overcame the lady in the circle and, opening her mouth, she gave a very loud scream, which reverberated all through the castle."

The spell was broken. The sky darkened and a violent storm erupted; the lake waters rose and the castle and everyone inside sank beneath them for ever.

HEALING CHARMS

The supernatural powers that all wizards must possess have traditionally included the ability to heal.

Magical medicine was first identified in Egypt. It was based on the central belief that anyone affected by illness was the prey of a negative force, or a demon. The doctor-magician would prepare the necessary medications and then empower them with a spell in order to make them more effective.

Many ancient Egyptian healing spells have been preserved. Afflictions of the head were regarded as particularly serious, because the head was considered to contain the doors of life. Even the gods were not immune from headaches and the story of Horus struck down by a bad migraine had to be recounted by a doctor-magician seven times as he treated a patient with the same complaint by rubbing ointment into the hands, body, and feet.

A similar approach was employed by magical healers in the Middle Ages, but they incorporated holy names or

passages from the Bible into their charms. The Christian Church condemned such actions as sorcery.

This traditional charm to stop a patient bleeding is based on a pseudo-biblical event:

"To be sed 3 times or if the case be bad 9 times and the Lords praier before & after holding your rithand on the place and marck the place thus + with your midel finger: Our Saviour Jesus Crist was borne in Bethalem was Baptsed of Jon in the river of Jordan. God commanded the water to stop & it stopped so in his name do I command the blood to Stop that runs from this orrafas vain or vaines as the water Stoped in the river of Jordan in the name of the Father Stop blud in the name of the son stop blood in the name of the holeygst not a drop more of blud proceduth Amen Amen Amen."

Healing charms are still regarded as one of the most important functions of modern magic and a wide variety of techniques are used. The magical power of magnetism is one such technique and is based on the ancient belief that a natural magnet, or lodestone, was a living spirit and that it could attract illness out of a patient if it was passed counterclockwise over the problem area.

The many benefits of herbs are acknowledged in modern medicine, and herbs were essential in magic healing. Cloth "poppets" filled with a selection of healing herbs are still used in magic rituals. They are tied to the afflicted area and a healing incense stick of frankincense or myrrh is circled counterclockwise over the image to remove the pain.

The yellow-flowered wild plant St John's Wort was commonly believed to possess the power not only to heal many different ailments—it is still taken as a herbal medicine to cure depression—but also to keep evil witches and wizards at bay.

The herb is most commonly linked with festivals marking Midsummer's Eve. According to British folk legend, countryfolk traditionally hung a bunch of St John's Wort over their front door to keep out evil magic on Midsummer's Eve. That was also the evening before the day of the Feast of St John the Baptist, after whom the plant was named, and the time when the herb was believed to be at its most potent.

A Wicca healing necklace can be created by following these instructions:

'Take three lengths of blue cord or string, approximately two feet long. Sit in your magick circle and braid the strands together. As you braid, chant the following while putting your intent into the cord or string:

Infuse these cords, send healing power, have it grow with every hour.'

Repeat the chant until you have finished braiding. Then say:

This is my will, so mote it be!'

CROCKS OF GOLD

Gold was revered by alchemists as the Sun; it was the magical elixir of youth and vitality. Alchemists dedicated their lives to finding a way to transmute base metals into gold, but despite many claims to have succeeded, no proof exists and in reality the correct spell has proved as illusory as the crock of gold that lies at the end of the rainbow.

The seventeenth-century British philosopher Francis Bacon, however, was not only convinced that it was possible to make gold, he actually described how to do it. Like others, though, there is no evidence that his method worked:

"Let there be a Small Furnace made, of a Temperate heat; For the Materiall, take Silver, which is the Metall that in Nature Symbolizeth most with Gold; Put in also, with the Silver, a Tenth Part of Quick-Silver, and Twelfth Part of Nitre, by weight; And so let the Worke be continued by the Space of Sixe Monthes, at the least. I wish also, that there be, at some times, an Injection of some Oyled Substance; such as they use in Recovering of Gold, which by Vexing with Separations hath beene made Churlish: And this is, to lay the Parts more Close and Smooth, which is the Maine Work. For Gold is the Closest of Metals."

Wizards not wishing to resort to their laboratories to create gold could tap into the creative energy of Mother Nature to increase their wealth. This traditional spell requires a single coin in order to work, but promises to yield a dozen more:

"The hollyhock blooms in Summer,
Its seeds in Autumn fall:
Then, in a folded paper,
Save them, gather them all—
The loose seeds,
The brown seeds,
The dry seeds,
The round seeds,
The seeds like tarnished pennies
That pay for the blossoms tall;
Bury their rusty treasure
Next to a southern wall—
With a mint coin,
An ancient coin,
A silver coin,
A copper coin:
By Spring your wealth shalt measure
Twelve times this sowing small."

multiplying. See it piling up, one coin on top of another. After a few minutes of this concentration, speak the following words:

'When the grey owlet has three times hoo'd,
When the grinning cat has three times mewed,
When the toad has croaked three times in the wood,
At the red of the Moon may this money be good.'

Sit for a few minutes and concentrate further on the silver multiplying. Repeat the incantation again and then a third time. Blow out the candles—first the left and then the right. Repeat this ritual every Wednesday for three weeks."

The following, more modern, magic ritual can also be practiced to make money:

"Sit cross-legged on the floor. Burn incense throughout the ritual. Take a silver half-dollar and wrap it in a piece of orange paper. Orange is the color of attraction. Set it before you on the floor. Stand two green candles, one on each side of the money, and light them. Concentrate on the wrapped silver and see in your mind's eye the silver

POWER AND INFLUENCE

The successful wizard is all-powerful. Although most ordinary mortals fall short of this achievement, we can but aspire to great wizardry, and a host of magical spells exist to speed us on our way to omnipotence.

An important first step is to ensure that the magic you are practicing is working to the utmost limit of its capabilities. By uttering this twenty-first-century chant while stirring your potion, for example, you are likely to increase its potency—and yours:

"Bubble, bubble, toil and trouble,
Strengthen this potion on the double.
Empower this magick, send it fast,
And it harm none, make it last."

Having firmly established your magical power-base, you can proceed to cast specific spells to advance your social standing. The following traditional ritual can be employed, for example, to obtain the job you have always coveted:

"When night has fallen fully,
Raise one candle's fire
And write on virgin paper
All that you desire;
If any man can aid you,
There inscribe his name,
Followed by these others
For Power, Skill and Fame
HELIMAZ
FERIDOX
SOLIDAR
Brush every word thereon
With a ragged crust of bread;
Then shred the paper, soak it
In water tinted red;
Wring it, press it small
As a lump of sodden dough —
Fling it from the house
As far as it will go."

If a bit of good luck is all that is needed to get on in life, then this Wicca spell can be used to make your own lucky stone:

"Take a white stone, an Apache's tear, or another stone that correlates with luck. Mix some lucky oil—cinnamon, cypress, or lotus oil, or some combination of the three—with a base, such as almond or grape-seed oil. Anoint the stone with the oil and charge it with this chant:

Into this stone before my eyes,
Bless thee, and charge thee my power to rise.
Enhance this stone with luck for me,
This is my will, so mote it be!"

JOHN DIMOND AND HIS GRANDDAUGHTER

*T*he ability to cast magic can be inherited, as the extraordinary powers possessed by two eighteenth-century American wizards, John Dimond and his granddaughter Molly Pitcher, testify.

It was Dimond's strange behavior that first caused his neighbors in the seaside town of Marblehead, Massachusetts, to suspect that they had a magician in their midst. As a young man, he would sometimes be seen to fall into deep trances, often lasting several days, from which he would emerge gifted with the uncanny power to foretell future events.

When Dimond purchased a dense thicket next to the old cemetery, and was overheard talking to the Devil there, locals were convinced he was a wizard and named him the "Marblehead Magician."

The accuracy with which Dimond could predict the future, however, meant that he was more often consulted than shunned. Happy to oblige the townsfolk, Dimond would gain the necessary information in a state of deep trance and was reputed to have solved many local crimes and recovered stolen objects through means of his supernatural powers.

But such powers paled beside the Marblehead Magician's mastery of the elements. Not only could Dimond divine storms at sea, he could also summon them. Locals believed that he communed with the spirits of those buried in the old cemetery in order to foretell the coming of a squall. Sea captains fortunate enough to find favor with him claimed to have heard his voice directing them away from the eye of the storm and guiding them to safer waters. Standing among the gravestones, Dimond roared directions to them over the land and water. Woe betide any sea captain who crossed him, however, for they would suffer his evil curse.

Legend tells how Dimond conjured a dreadful storm in order to kill his enemy Micah Taylor, captain of the "Kestrel." One clear blue day he was heard chanting magic from the old cemetery to summon the squall in which Taylor and everyone else on board the ill-fated ship drowned.

The Marblehead Magician's wizard granddaughter Molly Pitcher was equally feared and revered both in Massachusetts and beyond. Like Dimond, she possessed the ability to foretell future events, and would also act as a guardian angel to those in difficulty at sea. She, too, was known to curse a sea captain she disliked—sending them to a watery grave. Indeed, such was her reputation that no one would crew a ship sailed by anyone known to have crossed her.

Pitcher's most memorable magic feat was solving a famous murder in the nearby town of Concord. Baffled by the crime, the police consulted the local wizard. She fell into a deep trance, in which she not only revealed how the crime had been committed but also named the murderer. The guilty man subsequently confessed.

JOHN DIMOND

DAWN RAIDS

The guarding of doorways and gateways has always been an important part of magical protection. The threshold has traditionally had a powerful symbolical significance: it represents the boundary between belonging and not belonging, between safety and danger.

Just as a wizard inscribed protective symbols within a magic circle to strengthen its defences, so a frightened householder would use certain markings on his threshold to keep evil out of his home.

Evil magicians intent on entering a household could employ a particularly ghoulish talisman, the "Hand of Glory," to overcome any resistance. The "Hand of Glory" had to be the severed hand of a freshly hanged murderer, preserved by means of a complicated magic recipe. A candle made from the corpse's fat was inserted into the hand which, when lit and carried into any house, was guaranteed to send the occupants into a deep enchanted sleep.

Anyone wishing to fortify their threshold was alternatively advised to create a pattern of "a border of crosses between two lines; a series of vandykes with or without a circle in the wide part of each vandyke; two large crosses divided by a vertical line." A border of loops could also be added but "it had to be done straight round in an unbroken chain" in order to keep the Devil away.

Magical traps could also be set to catch evil spirits intent on causing harm within a home. To be sure of catching the demon, a householder could set a "cleft blackthorn stave with a lighted candle" in front of the trap to lure it in. The instructions for the successful trapping and disposal of a harmful spirit ran thus:

"Make a sprite trap out of a blackthorn stave and copper wire that has never carried electricity. Bind the wire to the stave with red thread and mark it with a D rune. Set it at the entrance to a home where disturbance takes place at night. When the trap has ensnared the spirit, remove it and cut the thread with a consecrated knife. Put the thread into a prepared witch bottle and say:

Thread, tie up this sprite,
Free us from its spite,
Tangel up the bane,
Let not a small piece remain,
Ka!'

Cork the bottle and seal it with red wax. Bury it and plant a thorn bush on the site."

Salt has always been central to spell-casting because it is revered as the one absolutely pure substance. It was traditionally scattered around thresholds as a protection against evil spirits and is still used in homes where magic is practiced. This is the most popular method of fortification:

"Dissolve the salt in water that has been placed in a clear glass container in Sun and waxing moonlight for twenty-four hours. Sprinkle the mixture in the four corners of every room and around the boundaries of your home, and your garden if you have one."

Number Magic

Wizards believe that numbers contain magical powers that can be invoked by using certain sacred ratios and shapes. Each number has a particular significance that must be fully understood when casting spells. These are the magic meanings of 0 to 9:

0
Time and Space without limit; the external circle without beginning or end.

1
Unity; the first manifestation of creative light that will multiply into millions of unique parts, each separate and yet containing the power of the first.

2
Duality; the mother/anima principle and the father/animus.

3
The Trinity and the Sacred Triangle; fertility and creation and balance.

4
The Square; the physical and material world; the most stable of numbers.

5
The Quintessence; the fifth element created from and unifying the other four: earth, air, fire, and water.

6
The Six Days taken to create the Earth.

7
Perfection; a combination of numbers three and four.

8
Balance; associated with prosperity and authority.

9
The number of initiation; the last of the single numbers, it brings the sequence to a close.

One of the most potent combinations of numbers is expressed in "magic squares," in which lines of numbers within a square all add up to the same number, whether read horizontally, vertically, or diagonally.

This numerical pattern is commonly used in magic:

Magical numbers correspond to specific letters of the alphabet and to certain colors. This is the most common magical formula:

1	AJS	Red
2	BKT	Orange
3	CLU	Yellow
4	DMV	Green
5	ENW	Blue
6	FOX	Indigo
7	GPY	Violet
8	HQZ	Silver
9	IR	Gold

By using these associations, wizards are able to calculate their magical names from their given names, and also to use their personal number combinations to find their primary power colors. All these discoveries are vital sources of empowerment.

Counting is, itself, believed to be a magic art that can be turned to one's advantage. It could be used in healing charms and was considered an effective method of curing warts, for example. Your warts would simply disappear, it was claimed, if you simply counted them and told a stranger the total number.

The most notorious magical number is 666. This was the number of the name of a "Great Beast" that would rule the Earth, according to the Book of Revelations in the Bible. The twentieth-century wizard Aleister Crowley styled himself the "Great Beast 666." He also created what he believed to be the ultimate word of power based on number magic: "AUGMN." Crowley described it as "the Magical Formula of the Universe as a reverbatory engine for the extension of Nothingness through the device of equilibrated opposites."

DAYS OF RECKONING

Those unwilling to carry out so much elaborate planning, however, can cast their spells at the times traditionally reckoned to be most conducive to magic.

Midnight is the "witching hour." It represents the deepest point of negativity—a time when all manner of demons may be abroad.

The most magical time to be born is midnight on a Friday. Anyone born at this time was gifted with the ability to see spirits and had power over the "evil eye." This spell to summon the queen of the fairies was most effective if chanted at midnight on a Friday:

"Micol o tu micoll regina pigmeorum deus Abraham: deus Isaac: deus Jacob; tibi benedicat et omnia fausta danet et concedat Modo venias et mihi moremgem veni. Igitur o tu micol in nominee Jesus veni cito ters quatur beati in qui nomini Jesu veniunt veni Igitur o tu micol in nomine Jesu veni cito qui sit omnis honor laus et Gloria in omne aeternum. Amen Amen."

Midnight on Halloween was the time to glimpse your true love, according to this traditional spell:

"Eat an apple at midnight on All halloween, and without looking behind you, gaze into a mirror, you will see the face of your future husband or wife."

There is a favorable time for every spell to be cast. A wizard should ideally co-ordinate his or her magic with the correct time of day, the appropriate season and the most auspicious movements of the planets in order to enhance its effect.

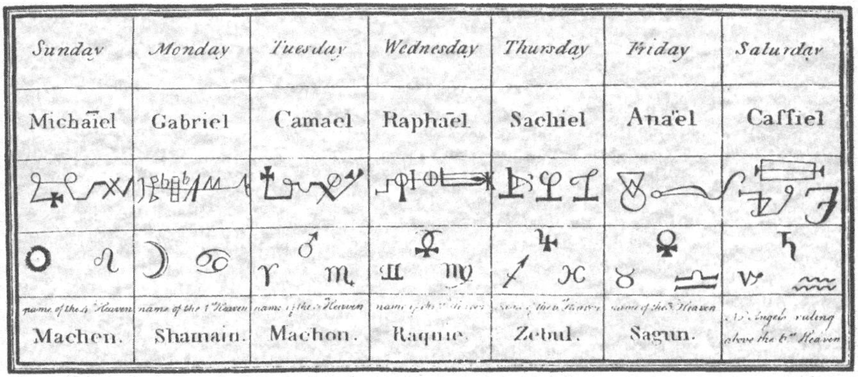

Sunday	Monday	Tuesday	Wednesday	Thursday	Friday	Saturday
Michael	Gabriel	Camael	Raphael	Sachiel	Anaël	Caffiel
name of the 4. Heaven	name of the 1.st Heaven	name of the Heaven	name of the Heaven	name of the Heaven	name of the Heaven	Archangel ruling above the 6th Heaven
Machen.	Shamain.	Machon.	Raqnie.	Zebul.	Sagun.	

Midsummer Eve is the true night for love. It would be a brave woman now, however, who followed this magical procedure to meet the man of her dreams:

"Go to the churchyard and wait for the stroke of twelve. Carry a bunch of rose leaves and a herb, such as rosemary. When the clock strikes, run around the church scattering the leaves and singing softly:

'Rose leaves, roses leaves, rose leaves I strew,
he that will love me,
Come after me now.'"

Each day of the week has its particular astrological and mythological meaning and wizards look at the cycle of the week when planning their magic in order to select the optimum time. Sunday is a good day to focus on health; Monday is best for fertility issues; Tuesday is right for money and leadership; Wednesday is propitious for divination; Thursday should be set aside for spells relating to prosperity; Friday is for love spells; and Saturday is for binding spells.

A powerful wizard, however, can control time itself and need not be bound by such limitations. This modern spell promises to accelerate time:

"Light three candles and place them on an altar. Create a circle and mark it with roses. Then recite these words:

'Winds of time gather round,
Give me wings to speed my way.
Rush me on my journey forward,
Let tomorrow be today.'"

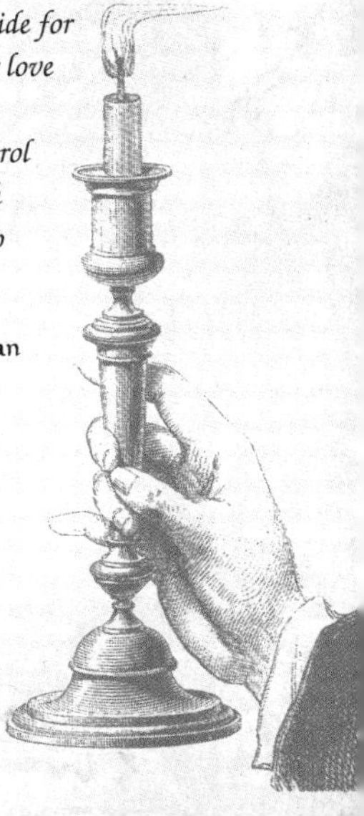

BINDING SPELLS

The tying and untying of knots is used to bind and release energy in many spells. The wizards of ancient Egypt believed that a magic knot was the point of convergence of the forces that unite the divine and the human worlds. A knot tied on Earth was also tied in heaven.

The awesome power of the magic knot has persisted through the centuries. In sixteenth-century France, couples living in Languedoc were so frightened that a knotting spell for castration would be cast on them as they wed, that less than ten weddings in every one hundred were performed in church. The spell they feared most was that cast by a sorceress, who would slip unseen into the church during a wedding ceremony and stand behind the groom:

"She knotted a thread, threw a coin on the ground and chanted:

'Whom God hath joined together
Let the Devil separate;
Sara till these knots be undone.'"

Wizards can control the wind by means of magic knots—but they must be paid for their efforts by those seeking their help:

"When three knots are tied with magic,
The wind is bound up in them.
Untying the first
Brings a fine breeze
Untying the second
Brings a high wind
Untying the third
Brings a tempest."

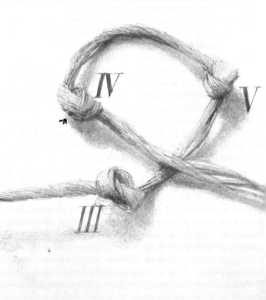

Knots are still central to magic ritual. In this twenty-first-century spell, which can be used to empower the desired object, the magic is completed with the tying of the ninth knot. In further variants, the spell is effected by the untying of the knots, one at a time over a period of nine days, or by tying the knotted cord into a circle:

"By knot of one this string I tie,
Let the magick begin, don't let it die.
By knot of two it will come true,
Whether I make it for me or you.
By knot of three it comes to be,
The magick will happen as you will see.
By knot of four my message will soar,
Up to the gods whom we adore.
By knot of five the magick's alive,
It will happen, it will survive.
By knot of six it will be fixed,
The power increasing as the clock ticks.
By knot of seven this spell I'll leaven,
As the message is carried up to the heavens.
By knot of eight it will not wait,
The magick will happen it won't be late.
By knot of nine my magick will shine,
It is my will placed in this rhyme."

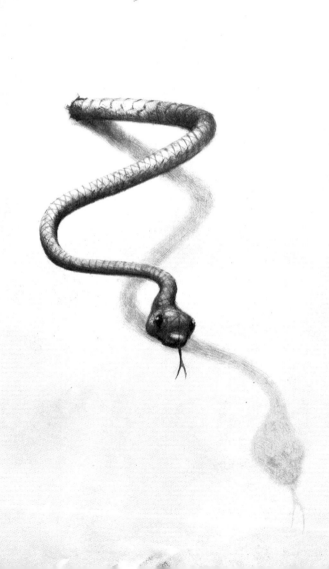